Anonymous

Topical history notes on English, Greek and Roman history : for the Matriculation Examination in the University of Toronto, and Junior Leaving Examinations in High Schools and Collegiate Institutes

Anonymous

Topical history notes on English, Greek and Roman history : for the Matriculation Examination in the University of Toronto, and Junior Leaving Examinations in High Schools and Collegiate Institutes

ISBN/EAN: 9783337157418

Printed in Europe, USA, Canada, Australia, Japan

Cover: Foto ©Paul-Georg Meister /pixelio.de

More available books at **www.hansebooks.com**

The W. J. Gage Co's Educational Series

TOPICAL HISTORY NOTES

ON

ENGLISH, GREEK AND ROMAN HISTORY

FOR THE

Matriculation Examination in the University of Toronto, and Junior Leaving Examinations in High Schools and Collegiate Institutes.

TORONTO:
THE W. J. GAGE COMPANY (LTD.)
1896.

PREFACE.

This book has been prepared to enable students to qualify more fully for the examinations in History for Matriculation to the University of Toronto, and the corresponding High School and Departmental examinations for teachers' non-professional certificates.

The notes may be used in connection with any larger Histories, and will be of great advantage to students in two ways: first, by giving them a comprehensive general view of the history of England, Greece and Rome before studying it in detail; and second, in reviewing the leading facts rapidly and definitely in preparing for examinations.

A TOPICAL ANALYSIS
OF
ENGLISH HISTORY.

FIRST TOPIC.

ENGLAND BEFORE THE ENGLISH CAME.

1. The original inhabitants of England were a barbarous race called Britons.
2. The Britons were first invaded by the Romans under Julius Cæsar, 55 B.C.; and the Romans took possession of the island under Agricola, A.D. 78.
3. The Romans remained in England for more than three hundred years, and began to leave it A.D. 410.
4. They built good roads, and two walls across the northern part of England. They founded several towns and introduced agriculture into England. They also introduced Christianity to a limited extent.

SECOND TOPIC.

CONSTITUTIONAL GROWTH IN ENGLAND BEFORE THE HANOVERIAN PERIOD

1. **Under the English.**
   1. The English people had developed the idea of representative government before they came to England.
   2. They worked out the foundation principles of municipal government and trial by jury. Two English kings, Alfred the

Great and Edward the Confessor, issued general laws for the guidance of the people.
3. The English at first divided England into seven kingdoms, but these were united into one by Egbert in 827.
4. Before the Normans came the English had the elements of a parliament called the Witenagemot, and municipal government in burghs, townships and shires.

2. Under the Normans.

1. The Feudal system, introduced by the Normans, took away the liberty of the people to take part in governing themselves, and made the kings absolute.
2. Free charters were, however, given to some cities and towns, with power to control their own affairs.
3. Henry I. established courts, and gave a charter which restored some of their liberty to the people.

3. Under the Angevins.

1. During the two and a half centuries of Angevin rule, great advance was made in constitutional growth.
2. The Feudal system was overthrown.
3. Henry II., one of the best kings that ever reigned in England, founded the system of courts that still exists, and re-established trial by jury.
4. The barons in the reign of John tired of the absolutism of kings, and forced the king at Runnymede to grant the Great Charter (Magna Charta).

Its chief provisions were:
   (a) That the king should not impose unjust taxes.
   (b) That the King sell no right or justice, nor deny or delay either of them.
   (c) That freemen should have full protection by law, and should not be seized, imprisoned, outlawed, dispossessed, or in any way brought to ruin, save by legal judgment of their peers.
   (d) That municipal privileges and greater freedom should be granted to the towns

5. The kings did not like to carry out the provisions of the Great Charter, but the barons under Simon de Montfort succeeded in getting a council established, by the Provisions of Oxford, to assist the king in governing the kingdom.
6. De Montfort wished more than this, however, and having secured a victory over the king, he called two representatives of the common people from every borough to a parliament in 1265. This was the real foundation of the House of Commons. De Montfort was killed, however, soon after he called his first parliament, and the commoners were not called again for thirty years. They have met regularly since 1295. At first parliament met in four departments, but since the time of Edward III. there have been two houses, as at present.
7. The power of parliament increased so rapidly that it deposed two of the Angevin kings.

4. Under the Lancastrians and Yorkists.
1. The Lancastrians were directed by Parliament.
2. The aristocracy became alarmed at the increase of voters among the common people, and passed laws prohibiting voting by the peasantry.
3. The Wars of the Roses destroyed the baronage, and Edward IV. was able to shake off the control of parliament, and establish the New Monarchy, which lasted till it was overthrown by Cromwell.

5. Under the Tudors.
1. The Tudors ruled without attention to the constitution. The kings were too strong for the barons. The leaders of the Church, instead of holding the kings in check, as they had done during the Angevin period, were tools to aid the kings in their tyranny; and the people, as a whole, had not yet developed their power. "The Tudor tyranny" was a dark period for the constitution.

6. Under the Stuarts.
1. The love of freedom that the English brought with them never died out. It was checked by the great power of the Norman

kings, but it revived quickly as the amalgamation of the English and Normans took place under the Angevins, and became strong enough even to depose two kings. Again it was checked by the destruction of the barons and the corruption of the Church during the Wars of the Roses, but it retained its vitality through the Tudor Tyranny, and in the Stuart period broke through the kingly bondage, and placed a check on kingly power that can never be removed.

The Barons and the leaders of the Church forced John to grant the Great Charter; but the people themselves overthrew the despotism of the Stuarts, and restored the liberties that had been taken away by the Yorkists and Tudors.

2. The Habeas Corpus Act, passed in 1679, provided:
 (a) That no prisoner, charged with a criminal offence, could be kept in prison more than twenty days without trial.
 (b) That judges in any court might issue a writ demanding a prisoner for trial.
 (c) That the Act should apply to the Colonies.

3. The Bill of Rights was really a modern Magna Charta. It was passed in 1689, and provided that without the consent of Parliament:—
 (a) No law could be made or repealed.
 (b) No taxes could be levied.
 (c) No standing army could be kept in time of peace.

The Bill of Rights provided also that parliament should be held frequently, and that it should be free from outside control.

4. The Act of Settlement provided that all future sovereigns of England must be Protestants.

5. Responsible Party Government was established in the reign of William and Mary. The Cabinet or Ministry must resign unless they are supported by a majority of the representatives of the people in the House of Commons.

6. The Parliaments of England and Scotland were united in 1707. The two countries had the same king from the time of James I. The Act of Union gave Scotland forty-five members in the Commons and sixteen in the House of Lords.

THIRD TOPIC.

GENERAL PROGRESS OF THE ENGLISH PEOPLE BEFORE THE HANOVERIAN PERIOD.

1. **Under the English Kings.**
    1. When the English came to England they were divided into three classes: the lowest or slaves, a middle class, who were free; and the nobles or earls.
    2. During the English period the slaves obtained their freedom.

2. **Under the Normans.**
    1. Towns and cities grew rapidly.
    2. Wealth increased.
    3. Manufactures increased largely by the aid of capital brought into the country by the Jews.
    4. Architecture improved.
    5. The Feudal system was established.

3. **Under the Angevins.**
    1. The overthrow of the Feudal system.
    2. The religious movement of the Friars, accompanied by habits of thrift and order in the people.
    3. The teaching of Wyclif and the love of freedom that followed it.
    4. The general explanation of laws to the people.
    5. The introduction of tenant farming instead of feudal farming, which freed the laboring classes.
    6. The attempt to reduce laborers again to serfdom, by the Statutes of Laborers, forbidding them to leave the parish in which they lived, and compelling them to accept very low wages.

7. The first great labor agitations, led by John Ball and Wat Tyler, showed that even the laboring classes were awakening to a consciousness of their right to greater freedom.

4. Under the Lancastrians and Yorkists.

1. Small land-holders vastly increased owing to the destruction of the baronage.
2. The people began to take a deeper interest in political affairs.
3. Learning was neglected, owing to the long civil wars, but the printing press began to prepare the masses for a forward educational movement.

5. Under the Tudors.

1. The mass of liberated laborers, set free by the overthrow of the Feudal system, required a great deal of careful attention in order to harmonize their altered condition with the social conditions of the country. Poor Laws were passed in Elizabeth's reign to settle, so far as possible, the questions arising in connection with laborers.
2. Manufactures and farming were widely extended, and the sturdy beggars got work.
3. England's commercial supremacy began to be felt.
4. The East India Company obtained its charter.
5. The Royal Exchange was established.
6. These improvements were made chiefly during the reign of Elizabeth.

6. Under the Stuarts.

The people, during this period, continued to advance, chiefly along the lines of political and religious freedom. The great number of able leaders that came from the middle classes shows that the people themselves were developing rapidly. Cromwell, Hampden, Pym, Eliot, Milton, were among the first fruits of the co-ordination of educational development and English freedom. The people now realized the equality of man, and their future development rested on educational and commercial advancement.

FOURTH TOPIC.

THE INFLUENCE OF THE CHURCH AS AN ELEMENT OF NATIONAL LIFE BEFORE THE HANOVERIAN PERIOD.

1. **Under the English.**

   The English worshipped several gods when they first came to England.
   2. Christianity was introduced about 600 by Augustine, Aidan and Cuthbert.
   3. Before the close of the English period great ecclesiastical statesmen had begun to direct the affairs of state.

2. **Under the Normans.**

   The English prelates were dismissed by William the Conqueror, and he appointed others over whom he retained absolute power.
   In the reign of William II. Anselm, the leader of the Church, opposed the king, and freed the Church from kingly control.

3. **Under the Angevins.**

   1. Henry II. determined to make the Church submit to the king. He was opposed by a very powerful prelate, Thomas Beket. Henry won.
   2. In the beginning of John's reign the clergy determined to become free from the king. The Pope made appointments in the English Church without consulting the king. John refused to recognize these appointments, and for five years defied the Pope. He surrendered at length most abjectly.
   3. The Friars caused a great religious awakening among the poorer classes during this period.
   4. The preaching of Wyclif led to a revolution in the minds of the English people in regard to religious freedom. Wyclif was really the first teacher of Protestantism in England.

4. Under the Lancastrians and Yorkists.
1. The Lollards (Wyclifites) were persecuted.
2. The Church increased in wealth but decreased in spiritual power.

5. Under the Tudors.
1. Henry VIII. denied the supremacy of the Pope, and proclaimed himself head of the Church.
2. The monasteries were destroyed by Henry VIII.
3. The Bible was translated into English.
4. Protestantism spread rapidly throughout England. The teaching of the followers of Wyclif, the spread of learning, the translation of the Bible, and the quarrel of Henry with the Pope, all combined to promote the propagation of Protestant principles. In the reign of Edward VI. the forty-two articles of the English Church were issued, and during the reign of Elizabeth the English Church was established on nearly its present system.
5. Many persecutions marred the Tudor period.

1. Cromwell (Thomas) destroyed the monasteries during the reign of Henry VIII.
2. Protestants were persecuted under Mary.
3. In Elizabeth's reign many Jesuits and their followers were put to death for plotting to secure the throne for Mary Queen of Scots.

6. Under the Stuarts.
1. The Puritan movement was the most important religious movement of the Stuart period. The Puritans were Protestants who wished to reform abuses and simplify the forms of worship in the English Church. They gained political supremacy under Oliver Cromwell. Their political supremacy ended with the rule of Cromwell, but their moral influence is felt still.
2. Roman Catholics and Protestants struggled hard for supreme power during the Stuart period. Finally Protestantism became thoroughly aroused by a plot to blow up the Houses of Parliament, and kill the king and members of parliament,

and by the ultra-Romanism of James II., and the result of the awakening, was the invitation of William of Orange to England, and the passage of the act of settlement which requires that all future rulers of England must be Protestants.

3. Archbishop Laud, in the reign of Charles I., persecuted Presbyterians and Puritans most cruelly.

4. Presbyterianism became the State Church of England by an agreement with the English parliament, on condition that Presbyterians would unite with parliament against Charles I. The English army, however, drove the Presbyterian members out of parliament, and speedily put an end to Presbyterianism as a State Church.

FIFTH TOPIC.

EDUCATION AND LITERATURE BEFORE THE HANOVERIAN PERIOD.

1. **During the English Period.**
The English people began to take a deep interest in education. Alfred the Great founded the University of Oxford.
Caedmon wrote poetry in English. Bede translated the Gospel of St. John into English.
Alfred the Great translated the Psalms and Æsop's fables into English, and arranged for the publication of the English Chronicle.
Owing to the many wars during the Norman, Angevin, Lancastrian, and Yorkist periods, the interest in education did not spread rapidly. With the introduction of printing, however, the interest increased, and the masses generally saw the advantages of education.
A great many grammar schools were opened during the Tudor period. In the latter half of the reign of Henry VIII. more grammar schools were established than for three centuries before. This revival was caused chiefly by the efforts of Colet and Erasmus.

The "new learning" gave great impulse to literature. The reign of Henry VIII. is marked by the founding of the English Middle Class schools, and the reign of Elizabeth is one of the brightest eras in English literature.

Sir Thomas Moore wrote in the time of Henry VIII. and during the reign of Elizabeth, Spencer, Shakspeare, Sydney, Bacon and many others laid the real foundation for English literature.

The English people passed through their greatest trial and achieved their grandest triumph in the struggle for religious liberty and political freedom during the Stuart periods. These struggles naturally affected the literature of the period. Great numbers of religious and political writings were issued. Many of them did not outlive the period in which they were written. Taylor's "Holy Living and Holy Dying," Bunyan's "Pilgrim's Progress," Baxter's "Saint's Rest," and Butler's "Hudibras," are still popular works.

The period produced able writers in other departments of literature. The most distinguished were Beaumont, Fletcher, and Ben Johnson, dramatists; Milton and Dryden, poets; Lord Clarendon and Bishop Burnett, historians; and Locke, a philosopher.

SIXTH TOPIC.

CHIEF WARS BEFORE THE HANOVERIAN PERIOD.

1. Under the English.

The chief wars during the English period were those caused by the invasions of the Danes and Normans. Alfred the Great saved England by driving out the Danes, but they returned a hundred years later and defeated the English. Danish kings ruled England 24 years—from 1017 to 1041.

When Edward the Confessor died without heirs, William of Normandy, the Conqueror, claimed that Edward had willed the English throne to him, and invaded England. He

defeated the English at Senlac (Hastings) 1066. Harold, the
Anglo-Saxon leader, who had been chosen king, was killed at
Senlac, and the Normans ruled for two years.

2. **Under the Normans.**

The English revolted from Norman rule during the second year
of the Conqueror's reign. He promptly suppressed the rebellion with great severity.
When Henry I., the third king, died, he gave the throne to his
daughter, but a great many wished to be ruled by a man,
and her cousin Stephen was chosen king by those who
objected to a queen. A civil war, in which Matilda was
aided by King David of Scotland, resulted, and lasted fourteen years. Stephen won the battle of the standard, and at
length Matilda agreed to let him retain the crown on condition that her son, Henry of Anjou, should be king after
Stephen's death.

3. **Under the Angevins.**

Henry II. conquered Ireland, and Edward I. conquered Wales.
John lost his French territory at the battle of Bouvines.
Edward III. claimed France because his mother was daughter of
the French king. The Black Prince, Edward's son, won
Cressy and Poitiers, and the French gave England Aquit-
taine and Calais, but Richard II., Edward's successor, lost
them.
Having subdued Ireland and Wales, the English tried to conquer
Scotland. Wallace and Bruce stubbornly opposed them.
Wallace was captured after eight years and put to death, but
Bruce avenged his death at Bannockburn, 1314. The war
was continued by Edward III. He won Halidon Hill, but
had to give up the Scotch war on account of the war in
France. The Scotch invaded England during Edward's
absence, but Queen Philippa defeated them at Neville's
Cross. Otterburn or Chevy Chase was fought between the
Douglases and Percys near the close of the Angevin period,
and won by the Scotch.
The great barons rebelled against the kings twice during the
Angevin period, first, when they forced John to grant the

Great Charter; Second, when Simon de Montford led them in demanding the representation of the people in the government of the country. He won at Lewes in 1264, but was defeated and killed next year at Evesham.

The rebellion of the nobles started ideas of freedom in the minds of the peasants too, and under Wat Tyler they revolted because they could not secure simple justice. Wat Tyler was killed by the Mayor of London. His death put an end to the revolt.

4. Under the Lancastrians and Yorkists.

Henry V. claimed the throne of France, and succeeded so well in his attempt at conquest that he was made Regent of France, and acknowledged to be heir to the throne. He died before the reigning king, and the war proceeded. Agincourt, 1415, was his most complete victory. The French were finally roused by Joan of Arc, a poor girl in the city of Orleans, who led the French armies so successfully that the English were unable to complete the conquest.

Jack Cade led a labor revolt in Kent after the French War. After meeting with considerable success he was murdered.

The two houses, York and Lancaster, fought for the throne with great bitterness for about sixteen years. The Yorkists were descended from the third son and the Lancastrians from the fourth son of Edward III. Henry VI. having no heirs till near the close of his reign, the Duke of York claimed the throne. The English nobility was divided into two parties. The Yorkists wore white roses, and the Lancastrians wore red roses, and so the war was named "The War of the Roses." After five years of fighting the king acknowledged York as his successor. Queen Margaret, who now had a son, objected to this arrangement. She raised an army, defeated York, and put him to death. Edward, the young Duke of York, proved to be a more dangerous foe than his father. He fought a great battle, and obtained a decisive victory at Towton in 1461. Twenty thousand Lancastrians, including most of their leaders, were killed, and King Henry was captured and put in prison where he was kept for nearly ten years. Edward was crowned as Edward IV. Margaret raised an army, chiefly French, but Edward again defeated her, and it seemed as if his position was secure. He quarrelled, however, with his best friend the Earl of Warwick, and Warwick became leader of the Lancastrians and drove the king from England. Henry was taken from prison for a short time, but Edward soon came back, and closed the war by defeating Warwick at Barnet (1471), and Margaret, who was on her way to join Warwick at Tewkesbury. Warwick was killed at Barnet, and the Lancastrian heir at Tewkesbury.

Edward V. was only thirteen years of age when he came to the throne. His Uncle Richard was appointed Protector. He laid plans to become king. He put the young king and his brother in prison, and had them murdered there. This roused great indignation throughout the country, and Henry Tudor, a Lancastrian, proposed to marry Elizabeth, the eldest sister of the murdered princes, and thus unite both Yorkists and Lancastrians against Richard. He defeated Richard at Bosworth field in 1485. Richard was killed on the field, and Henry became king.

5. Under the Tudors.

There were several unimportant wars during the Tudor period. In one of them the Scotch were defeated, and their king killed at Flodden, by Henry VIII. Queen Mary lost Calais in a French war. A brief civil struggle in favor of Lady Jane Grey ended in the triumph of Queen Mary.

But the most important war was that caused by the attempt of Philip of Spain to conquer England and overthrow Protestantism. He sent his invincible Armada, but it was defeated by the English, and afterwards almost entirely destroyed by a storm.

6. Under the Stuarts.

The Parliament began to demand liberty from the tyrannical rule of the kings early in the Stuart period. Led by Pym Hampden and Elliot, the Parliament finally came to a war with Charles I., who claimed the "divine right of kings."

The Parliament formed the "Solemn League and Covenant" with Scotland, and, under Cromwell, the Parliamentary army defeated the king at Marston Moor, 1644, and Naseby, 1645. In 1646 Charles surrendered. After two years in prison he was tried by Parliament and executed for making war on his own subjects. One hundred and forty of his friends were excluded from Parliament when the vote of condemnation was taken.

Rebellions in favor of royalty occurred, both in Scotland and Ireland, after the execution of Charles I., but Cromwell speedily settled both rebellions. The Scotch, under General Leslie, were defeated at Dunbar and Worcester, and the Irish submitted after the siege of Drogheda.

After William III. came to England, James II. raised an army in Ireland, but William scattered his army at the Boyne in 1689.

The English were at war three times with Holland during the Stuart period. The most important result of these was the cession of New York to the English.

William III. was not acknowledged king of England by Louis XIV. of France for nine years after he came to England. Louis took the part of James II. William showed wise generalship, and amid great difficulties, and with a smaller army, he compelled Louis to sue for peace, and recognize him as ruler of England. The chief events of the war were the great victory of the English over the French fleet at La Hogue, which compelled Louis to give up his plan for the invasion of England, and the capture of Port Royal from the French in Nova Scotia.

The greatest war of the Stuart period was the war of the Spanish succession. England, Holland, Austria and Germany (except Bavaria) supported the claim of the Emperor of Austria; France, Spain, and Bavaria supported the grandson of Louis XIV. The Duke of Marlborough led the army of England and her allies. He was a brilliant general, and won four great victories; Blenheim, 1704; Ramilies, 1706; Oudenarde, 1708; and Malplaquet, 1709. Gibraltar was taken by Sir Charles Rooke in this war.

SEVENTH TOPIC.

THE SEVEN YEARS' WAR.

1. French in America gradually making encroachments on the English. In India also they seek to drive out English traders. National jealousy aroused that only waits for occasion to manifest itself.
2. George II. as ruler of Hanover, is jealous of Prussia, with which his Ministers seek to be in alliance. Russia also jealous of Prussia. Maria Theresa passionately desires to get back Silesia.
3. In 1755 Maria Theresa joins in league with France, Spain, Russia and Saxony against Prussia. Negotiations very secret.
4. In spite of George II.'s opposition his Ministers make a treaty with Frederick of Prussia, providing for the neutrality of Prussia and Hanover in any contest between England and France. Treaty gives offence. Prussia and England have to fight the rest of Europe.
5. Course of Events. War opens disastrously. England unprepared. Port Mahon, in Minorca, lost. Admiral Byng retreats. Duke of Cumberland falls back before a French army and engages, by convention of Closter-Seven, to disband his forces. In America, French have possession of the Valley of the Mississippi. General despondency. "We are no longer a nation." Pitt comes to the front. His union with Newcastle. The tide of fortune turns. Plassey gives England control of Bengal (June, 1757). Frederick defeats the French at Rosbach (November, 1757). Soon after, at Leuthen, defeats the Austrians and clears Silesia of them. But a series of defeats reduces his fortunes to lowest point (1759). England, meanwhile, gains three great victories—Minden, Quiberon, Quebec. Death of George II. (1760). War continues. Capture of Pondicherry destroys the power of the French in India. France makes a new "Family Compact" with Spain. Pitt wishes to declare war with Spain

at once. George III. refuses. Pitt resigns. Lord Bute's administration. War declared against Spain, 1762. English capture Havannah and many Spanish Treasure-ships. Take also some islands of the French West Indies. Negotiations for peace (November, 1762). Peace of Paris (February, 1763).
6. Conditions of treaty :
   (a) England obtained Canada, Cape Breton, Nova Scotia, Louisiana, Dominica, St. Vincent and other islands in West Indies, Senegal, Minorca, the two Floridas (from Spain).
   (b) France got back Guadaloupe, Martinico, Belleisle.
   (c) Spain got Havana and the Phillippine Islands in exchange for the two Floridas and the Spanish possessions in North America.
   (d) Prussia did not lose any territory ; held Silesia.
7. General results of the war :
   (a) England becomes the head of a great Empire.
   (b) France is effectually checked in her aim to break up the unity of Germany.
   (c) The unity of Germany sprang from the victory of Rossbach.

EIGHTH TOPIC.

KINGLY POWER SINCE THE REVOLUTION.

(Beside T.L., students will do well to consult May's Constitutional History, and that of Prof. C. D. Yonge.)

1. "In outer seeming the revolution of 1688 had only transferred the sovereignty over England from James to William and Mary. In actual fact, it was transferring the sovereignty from the king to the House of Commons."—*G.*
2. Yet the personal influence of the king was very great. "William III. was his own Prime Minister, his own Foreign Minister, his own Commander-in-Chief. Queen Anne not only regularly presided at Cabinet Councils, but, occasionally attended debates in the House of Lords."—*T-L.*

3. The change brought about under George I.—He did not know enough English to preside at Cabinet meetings. He cared nothing for English politics. Similarly George II. "Having lent their names and authority to competent Ministers, they acted upon their advice, and aided them by all the means at the disposal of the Court."—*May.*
4. George III. attempts "*not only to reign but to govern.*" Circumstances favorable to his design: (a) He was born and educated in England; (b) He was personally popular; (c) He was possessed of a strong will and considerable talents for intrigue; (d) The Tory party were now loyal and earnest supporters of the king; (e) The Whig party was broken into factions; (f) The king was the fountain of honor; he could bestow honors, dignities, places and preferments.
5. Difficulties in the king's way: (a) His Ministers were responsible to Parliament for every act of their administration; (b) They had been so long accustomed to exercise the power of the Crown that they were reluctant to give it up; (c) The Whig families had for fifty years dispensed the patronage of the Crown, (d) The House of Commons was difficult to control in the king's interests.
6. Means adopted by the king to carry out his design: (a) The formation of a party, "The King's Friends"; (b) Persistent efforts to break up all parties that thwarted his will; (c) Dismissed as soon as possible the Ministers in power at his accession (Pitt and Newcastle); (d) Supported, with all the resources at his command, Lord Bute, who became his mouthpiece; (e) Interfered in the election of members of Parliament; (f) Employed bribery, etc., to gain adherents in the House of Commons; (g) Forced those Ministers who would not obey his will implicitly to resign or to sacrifice largely their convictions; (h) Dismissed from their offices those members of Parliament who opposed his favorite Ministers.
7. Relation of the king to the Ministers during his reign:
  (a) Pitt and Newcastle. Pitt too great to be subservient; Newcastle, no longer consulted in the dispensal of patronage, resigned after "numerous affronts."

(b) Bute—entirely subservient. Only eleven months in office. Intensely unpopular with the people (1763).

(c) Grenville—"differed as to their relative powers, but too well agreed in their policy, both arbitrary, impatient of opposition, and resolute in the exercise of authority." Chief acts of this Minister: (1) Proceedings against Wilkes; (2) The first taxation of America. King sought to dismiss him (early in 1765), but was unable to get any one to take office. At length (late in the same year), he could no longer endure the Grenville Ministry and dismissed it.

(d) Rockingham, leader of the Whig aristocracy, had recently been dismissed from his Lord-Lieutenancy for opposing the king. Relation of the king to this Minister suggested by his conduct in the matter of the repeal of the Stamp Act. "He (the king), resisted this measure in Council, but finding Ministers resolved to carry it, he opposed them in Parliament by the authority of his name, and by his personal influence over a considerable body of Parliamentary adherents." In July, 1766, they were ungraciously dismissed.

(e) Duke of Grafton.—Pitt as Earl Chatham, the ruling spirit of the Ministry for over two years, then, his health giving way, he resigned. Grafton's Ministry continued till 1770. Pitt, during his term of office, played into the king's hands by helping to break up parties. The Duke of Grafton, "partly from indolence and partly from facility, consented to follow the stronger will of his sovereign."

(f) Lord North. 1770-1782.—"That Minister, by principle a Tory, and favorable to prerogative—in character indolent and good-tempered, and personally attached to the king—yielded up his own opinions and judgment, and for years consented to be the passive instrument of the royal will. The persecution of Wilkes, the straining of parliamentary privilege, and the coercion of America, were the disastrous fruits of the Court policy. Throughout this administration the king staked his personal credit again the success of his measures, and regarded opposition to his Ministry as an act of disloyalty and their defeat as an affront to himself." May.

In 1780 a resolution was passed in the House of Commons declaring "that the influence of the Crown had increased, is increasing, and ought to be diminished." When the North Ministry was overthrown the king spoke of retiring to Hanover rather than submit to the limitation of his power which a change of Ministry would bring.

(g) Rockingham. — Policy distasteful to the king. "Its first principle was the concession of independence to America, which he had so long resisted; its second was the reduction of the influence of the Crown by the abolition of offices, the exclusion of contractors from Parliament, and the disfranchisement of revenue officers."—May. Ministry only a few months in office.

(h) Lord Shelburne. — In office only nine months. Trusted to maintain himself entirely by the king. Overthrown by a coalition of the followers of North and Fox.

(i) Duke of Portland. — North and Fox the real leaders. The king said, "to such a Ministry he never would give his confidence, and that he would take the first moment for dismissing them." Opportunity came in opposing Fox's India Bill.

(j) William Pitt (1783-1801). — The struggle between Pitt on the one side, and North and Fox on the other. Pitt triumphs. The king "had now a Minister, who, with higher abilities and larger views of State policy, had a will even stronger than his own. . . If the king was no longer his own Minister, as in the time of Lord North he had the satisfaction of seeing his own principles carried out by hands far abler than his own."—May. The influence of the Crown now greater than ever. Pitt resigned, 1801, owing to the king's persistent refusal to sanction a measure for the relief of Roman Catholics.

(k) Mr. Addington enjoyed the confidence and even the affection of the king.

(*l*) **Pitt's second Ministry.**—Pitt wished to have the assistance of Fox. The king resolved " not to admit Fox to his Councils, even at the hazard of a civil war." Pitt's lofty temper now distasteful to the king. Death of Pitt, 1806."

(*m*) **Lord Grenville and Fox.**—Ministry "maintained its ground so long as it was tolerated at Court, but when it ventured to offend the king's religious scruples it fell suddenly, like that of Pitt in 1801."

(*n*) Duke of Portland and Mr. Percival. King became insane, 1810.

8. Since the reign of George III. the direct personal influence of the sovereign has steadily declined.

NINTH TOPIC.

THE ENGLISH IN THE NEW WORLD.

1. **The War of American Independence.**
  A. **Causes.** (See in particular May.)
  1. To a considerable extent, the English colonies had been left very much to themselves. "In matters of imperial concern, England imposed her own policy; but otherwise left them free. Asking no aid from her, they escaped her domination. All their expenditure, civil and military, was defrayed by taxes raised by themselves."—*May.*
  2. In pursuance of his general policy George III. determined to make the colonies contribute to the general revenues of the government. Following are the arguments in favor of this determination:
      (*a*) Much of the national debt had been incurred in defence of the colonies.
      (*b*) Other States had been accustomed to enrich themselves by the taxation of their dependencies.

(c) Constitutional lawyers held that it was competent for Parliament to tax the colonies.
(d) Parliament had on many occasions passed acts providing for the levy of colonial import and export duties.

Arguments against:
(a) The colonies had had no voice in the wars by which England's debt had been incurred.
(b) The colonies had taxed themselves heavily for protection against the foes of the Mother Country with whom they had no quarrel.
(c) Granted that Parliament could make laws for government of the colonies, yet, by constitutional usage, taxes were always granted by the people through their representatives.

3. The Stamp Act passed in 1765. The colonies individually, and through representatives in a Congress, denied the right of Parliament to pass such an Act.

4. Act repealed by Rockingham administration in spite of the obstinate resistance of the king and his friends (1766). At the same time Declaratory Act passed, asserting the supreme power of Parliament over the colonies, " in all cases whatsoever."

5. George III. intensely annoyed by the repeal of the Stamp Act. Determined to seize the first opportunity to undo the "fatal compliance of 1766."

6. In 1767, Townshend, notwithstanding what had happened, imposed a variety of small customs' duties on the colonies. Another period of agitation, and Government withdrew all but a tax on tea (1769). Americans refuse to buy taxed tea.

7. Attack on tea-ships at Boston (1773) gives the king the opportunity for which he has been waiting.

8. King refuses to consider the question of compensation. Boston punished by having its port closed against all commerce. Massachusetts has its charter altered. Troops sent to "bring the Americans to their senses."

9. The colonies adopt the quarrel of Massachusetts. Hold a Congress (1774) to arrange joint action.
10. Lord Chatham (1775) brings forward a measure providing for the repeal of the late Acts, for the security of the colonial charters, the abandonment of the claim to taxation, and the recall of the troops. It is contemptuously rejected.
11. The Congress of delegates adopt measures for general defense, raise an army and put Washington over it.

B. Course of War.

1. 1775. Skirmish of Lexington, April 19th.
2. Battle of Bunker's Hill.
3. The British troops cooped up during the winter (1775-6) in Boston. In spring they withdraw to New York.
4. General Arnold makes a raid upon Canada.
5. The Southern colonies expel their governors.
6. 1776. Declaration of Independence, July 4th.
7. Howe gains the victory of Brooklyn. Washington forced to evacuate New York and New Jersey. Later gains some successes.
8. 1777. Burgoyne marches from Canada to seize the line of the Hudson; then, with the help of the army at New York, to cut off the New England States from the others. He finds himself confronted by General Gates. Surrenders at Saratoga (October).
9. Howe sails up the Chesapeake, defeats Washington at Brandywine, takes Philadelphia. Washington faces Howe's army at Valley Forge during the winter.
10. Chatham again tries to bring about a reconciliation—fails.
11. 1778. France and Spain conclude an alliance with the States. They declare war.
12. All hope of reconciliation passes away with the death of Pitt.
13. 1779. Gibraltar besieged. The Dutch join the league against England. In America the British Generals are successful in the South.

14. 1780. Lord Cornwallis captures Charlestown and plans other towns. The United States bankrupt.
15. 1781. Cornwallis surrenders to Washington at Yorktown.
16. Lord North resigns.
17. 1782. November. Preliminaries for peace signed.
18. 1783. Peace of Versailles.
    Conditions:
    (a) Independence of United States acknowledged.
    (b) France to get a share of the Newfoundland fisheries and Islands of St. Pierre and Miquelon.
    (c) Spain to get Minorca.
    (d) England to keep Canada and Newfoundland.

C. **Results.**
   1. "If it crippled for a while the supremacy of the English nation, it founded the supremacy of the English race."—G. A great English-speaking nation was established in America in which, on a wide scale, English law, English institutions, and English liberty began a new career.
   2. The Mother Country was taught some useful lessons from which, in her subsequent dealings, she profited. No further attempt was made to tax any of her colonies.

2. **Canada Under British Rule.**
   (Student may consult Withrow's History.)
   1. 1760-1761. Canada under a military government. The country divided into three jurisdictions—Quebec, Montreal, and Three Rivers.
   2. Indians dissatisfied with English rule. Pontiac's war.
   3. In 1764, Canada formally annexed to British possessions by royal proclamation. Government established. A Governor and Council. Representative institutions promised as soon as the country became ready for them. English law, and English methods of conducting judicial proceedings, introduced.

4. Dissatisfaction among the French. They are excluded from all offices, and treated as a conquered race. They dislike the English law and English tenure of land.
5. The Quebec Act (1774). Its provisions:
    (a) "Extended the bounds of the province from Labrador to the Mississippi, from the Ohio to the watershed of Hudson's Bay.
    (b) "Established the right of the French to the observance of the Roman Catholic religion, without civil disability, and confirmed the tithes to the clergy. Exempting, however, Protestants from their payment.
    (c) "Restored the French civil code, and established the English administration of law in criminal cases.
    (d) "Vested supreme authority in the Governor and Council, the latter being nominated by the Crown, and consisting for the most part of persons of British birth."—W.
6. Canada and the American Revolution. Canada invited to join in the revolt. French fairly satisfied with the concessions of the Quebec Act refuse, but are apathetic as to the result of the contest between Britain and her colonies. The Americans invade Canada (1775). Montreal occupied. Ineffectual siege of Quebec by Arnold. The Americans compelled to retire (1776). In 1777 Burgoyne invades New York from Canada. Importance of Treaty of Versailles to Canada.—"By its terms Canada was despoiled of the magnificent region lying between the Mississippi and the Ohio, and was divided from the new nation by the Great Lakes, the St. Lawrence, the watershed between the St. Lawrence and the Atlantic, and the St. Croix River."—W. The war, followed by an exodus of U.E. Loyalists to Canada—10,000 to Ontario alone.
7. The Constitutional Act (1791). The rapid development of what is now Ontario, since the American War, raised the question of its separation from Quebec.

(a) The Act "divided Canada into two portions by a line coinciding chiefly with the Ottawa River.
(b) "In Upper Canada, British law, both civil and criminal, and freehold land tenure, were introduced.
(c) "In Lower Canada the Seigneurial and French law, in civil cases, were retained.
(d) "In each province a government was constituted, consisting of an elective Legislative Assembly, and a Legislative Council and Governor appointed by the Crown.
(e) "One-seventh of the land was reserved for the use of the Crown, and one-seventh for the maintenance of the Protestant clergy."—W.

8. The War of 1812-15.

A. **Its Causes.**
1. Napoleon's "Berlin Decree," and the retaliatory British "Orders-in-Council" press heavily on American shipping. The American Non-Intercourse Act. Mutual exasperation.
2. Britain asserts her "right of search" for deserters from the navy.
3. The publication of the secret correspondence of a Captain Henry who had reported that New England was ready to secede from the Union.
4. A desire to annex the Provinces of British North America with the United States.

B. **Course of Events.**
1812.
1. War declared, June.
2. Sir Isaac Brock takes Fort Makinaw and secures the allegiance of the British.
3. The American plan of attack. Canada invaded at three points.
(a) General Hull crosses the Detroit River - Brock goes to meet him. He re-crosses. Brock follows. Hull surrenders.

(b) Van Ranselaer crosses the Niagara at Queenston. Battle of Queenston Heights. Death of Brock. The American force surrenders. Other American troops prevented from crossing.

(c) General Dearborn advances by way of Champlain. fails in an attack at Lacolle, and retires into winter quarters.

1813.
1. Both sides make extraordinary efforts to continue the war.
2. The Americans construct strong vessels for the lakes.
3. American plan—to conquer Upper Canada.

(a) Proctor captures Winchester and 500 Americans at French Town, Michigan. Later in the year is compelled to cross the Detroit River and fall back before General Harrison. Battle of Moravian Town (October), British defeated. Western Upper Canada in American power.

(b) Americans take York and Fort George, but are defeated at Stoney Creek and Beaver Dams. Sir George Prevost and Sir James Yeo attack Sackett's Harbor. Attack not so successful as it might have been from over-caution. In revenge, the Americans plunder and burn the town of York, but are defeated by Yeo when returning across the lake.

(c) An American force gathered (October) near Sackett's Harbor to advance against Montreal. Defeated at Chrysler's Farm.

(d) Another force invading Canada by way of Champlain. Defeated at Chateauguay.

(e) These defeats led the American Commander at Fort George to abandon it in December, after setting fire to every house in Niagara. In revenge for this the Canadians take Fort Niagara and ravage the whole frontier.

1814.
(a) The American General, Wilkinson, defeated (March) at Lacolle Mill by a force much smaller than his own.

(b) British troops defeated at Chippewa, but the Americans defeated at Lundy's Lane.
(c) A force under the over-cautious Prevost advanced against the Americans at Plattsburg, but failed to accomplish anything.

1815.
The British defeated in an attack on New Orleans.

C. Peace of Ghent, December, 1814.
1. Americans did not gain any territory. The adjustment of unsettled boundaries was left to a commission.
2. The "right of search" and the rights of neutrals were not mentioned in the treaty; the European War was now over.
3. An agreement made for a combined effort for the suppression of the slave traffic.

TENTH TOPIC.

THE GROWTH OF THE BRITISH EMPIRE IN INDIA.

(See Macaulay's Essay on Clive and Hastings.)

1. In 1760, British supremacy was established over Bengal, and over Southern India.
2. The work of organization followed that of conquest.
    (a) Clive's work as an organizer: (1) He organized the service of the East India Company in India; (2) he put down the trading of the Company's servants, and forbade their acceptance of gifts from the natives.
    (b) In 1767, he returned to England, and by unsparing denunciations of the misgovernment of Bengal attracted the attention of the government to India.
    (c) The Regulation Act, 1773:
        (1) Established a Governor-General and a Supreme Court of Judicature for all British possessions in India.
        (2) Prohibited judges and members of Council from trading.

(3) Forbade any receipt of presents from natives.

(4) Ordered that every act of the Directors should be signified to the government to be approved or disallowed.

(d) Clive's own career inquired into. He is censured, but the Commons unanimously vote "That Robert Lord Clive did at the same time render great and meritorious services to his country."

3. Hastings the first Governor-General. His administration, 1773–1785:

  (a) Established the direct rule of the East India Company over Bengal.
  (b) Organized afresh the system of government, respecting as far as possible the prejudices, feelings and habits of the natives.
  (c) Began deliberately the subjugation of all India to the British Crown.
  (d) Sold the services of the Company's army to crush the Rohillas.
  (e) Met and in the end defeated the Mahrattas (who were incited by the French).
  (f) Met the danger from Hyder Ali, whom Coote defeated at Porto Novo, 1781.
  (g) Annexed Benares.
  (h) Reduced Oude to virtual dependence.

4. The many unscrupulous acts of Hastings lead to his impeachment. His long and memorable trial, 1786–1795. The investigation of the character of his administration made it apparent that it was not advisable to permit a trading company to rule over so great a possession.

5. Mr. Fox's India Bill, 1783. "Proposed to transfer the political government (of India) from the directors of the Company, to a Board of seven Commissions. The appointment of the seven was vested in the first instance in Parliament, and afterwards in the Crown." Bill defeated in the Lords, the king exercising his influence for that purpose. The ministry requested to resign.

6. Mr. Pitt's India Bill, 1784. It "preserved in appearance the political and commercial powers of the Directors, while establishing a Board of Control, formed from members of the Privy Council for the approving or annulling of their acts." This dual method of governing India continued till 1858 when its government was vested directly in the Crown.

7. British rule only once seriously threatened during remainder of the period (1707 sq. Tippoo Sahib, successor to Hyder Ali in Mysore, vows to drive the English into the sea. Is killed at the storming of his capital, Seringapatam, and Mysore added to the British dominions.

ELEVENTH TOPIC.

THE ADMINISTRATION OF THE YOUNGER PITT.

A. The Circumstances under which he assumed power.

The king had contemptuously dismissed the coalition Ministry of North and Fox, and entrusted the formation of a Government to William Pitt. Pitt's followers were in a minority in the Commons. He was defeated again and again, but refused to resign. Meanwhile, the king was exercising his influence in Pitt's favour. The adverse majorities gradually dwindled down, and on the House being dissolved (March, 1784), and a new election taking place, an overwhelming majority was returned in favor of Mr. Pitt. (For constitutional principles involved in this struggle, see *May*, chap. I, pages 72, etc.)

B. Pitt's relation to the King.

The king trusted him because he had saved him from the power of the coalition. Pitt was no puppet in the king's hands, his will was stronger than his master's; yet the king never ceased to guard carefully the royal power. "He (George) had the satisfaction of seeing his own principles carried out by hands far abler than his own.

In prosecutions of the press, and the repression of democratic movements at home, the Minister was, perhaps, as zealous as the king; in carrying on war to crush democracy abroad, the king was more zealous than his Minister. They labored strenuously together in support of Monarchy all over the world, and respected too little the constitutional liberties of their own people."
—*May.*

C. Pitt's Foreign Policy.

1. "He was a 'peace minister' and a statesman, who saw that the best security for peace lay in the freedom and widening of commercial intercourse between nations."
—*G.*

2. Commercial Treaty of 1787 between England and France, framed on those principles. It enabled subjects of both countries to reside and travel in either without license or passport, did away with all prohibition of trade on either side, and reduced every import duty."—*G.*

3. The intimate connection between England and France, made the events of the French Revolution of 1789 of great interest in England. Pitt's attitude towards the Revolution—cool, but without distrust.

4. Besides his desire for peace, Pitt's policy in Eastern Europe led him to seek an alliance with France. Catharine of Russia had two objects in view: (*a*) the annexation of Poland; (*b*) the expulsion of the Turks from Europe. Austria was willing to join her in carrying out her plans. To defeat the designs of Russia and Austria, Pitt had renewed the old friendship of England with Prussia, and in 1789 entered into an alliance with Prussia and Holland to preserve the Turkish Empire. But Prussia had designs on Poland herself, and hence Pitt's anxiety for a French alliance.

5. Burke, alarmed at the doctrines of the French Revolution, had determined to make a continuance of peace between France and England impossible. Pitt struggled against the slowly-rising tide of public opinion until opposition was impossible, and war was declared 1793.

TOPICAL HISTORY. 31

6. Pitt an unsuccessful War Minister. He was at heart a
   Peace Minister; he was forced into the war; he was
   destitute of his father's power to arouse enthusiasm.
7. England joined the league against France, consisting of
   Austria, the Empire, Prussia, Spain, and Sardinia. During this war England accomplished nothing worthy of
   herself on land, but she kept her position as mistress of
   the sea. Her money was given lavishly to keep the continental armies in the field. She was paymaster of the
   coalitions.
8. This war at once gave Russia her opportunity. Poland
   was divided, Russia, Austria and Prussia each getting a
   share. Pitt was powerless to prevent it.
9. Throughout the war Pitt kept watching for an opportunity to bring it to a close. His attempt in 1796 was a
   failure owing to the elation of the French over the
   victories of Napoleon in Italy. No other opportunity
   offered during his first Ministry.
10. Pitt's later position was "one of almost tragic irony. An
    economist heaping up millions of debt, a peace Minister
    dragged into the costliest of wars, he is the very type of
    a baffled statesman."
11. Pitt was recalled to power 1804, during the period of the
    threatened French invasion. He succeeded in forming
    an alliance with Russia, Austria and Sweden, to resist
    French aggression. But the crushing defeat of the
    Austrians at Austerlitz killed him.

D. Pitt's Domestic Policy.

1. "His policy from the first was a policy of active reform,
   and he faced every one of the problems financial, constitutional, religious, from which Walpole had shrunk."
   —G.
2. FINANCIAL POLICY:
   (a) Smith's "Wealth of Nations" was the groundwork
       of his policy.
   (b) He was able to carry on the Government without
       making the taxes too oppressive.

(c) He proposed to pay off the national debt gradually
       by means of a sinking fund.
   (d) He reduced the customs duties to such an extent as
       to make smuggling unprofitable, yet the revenue
       increased.
   (e) He made (1787), a Treaty of Commerce with France.
   (f) He proposed free trade with Ireland, but this offer
       was rejected by the Irish Parliament.
   (g) He succeeded in bringing about free trade between
       England and Ireland immediately after the Union
       (1800).
   (h) Why he failed to do more: (1) He had to contend
       with the ignorance and prejudice of those who sup-
       ported him; (2) The breaking out of the French
       Revolution put a stop to his plans.
2. CONSTITUTIONAL POLICY:
   (a) The India Bill (1784). Pitt "left the (East India)
       Company in possession of their large powers, but
       subjected them to a Board of Control representing
       the Crown. The company were now accountable
       to Ministers in their rule; and Ministers, if they
       suffered wrong to be done, were responsible to Par-
       liament."—*May.*
   (b) The Bill "to amend the representation of the people
       of England in Parliament" (1785).
   (c) The Regency Bill (1789). George III. had become
       insane, and the Prince of Wales claimed the regency
       as a right. Pitt resisted the claim on the ground
       that Parliament alone had the right to appoint a
       regent.
   (d) The Constitutional Act (1791). Divided the Canadas
       and gave them self-government.
   (e) Supported Fox's Libel Bill (1792), which gave the
       jury the right to decide whether a publication is
       libelous or not.
   (f) Resisted the panic excited by the French Revolution,
       but moved (1794) for the suspension of the Habeas
       Corpus Act.

(g) Carried through the Act of Union between England and Ireland.
(h) Proposed (1801) to introduce in Parliament a Catholic Emancipation Bill, but the proposition met with the determined opposition of the king. This led Pitt to resign.

4. POLICY IN RELIGIOUS MATTERS. (See May, chap. XII.)
  (a) In 1787, 1789 and 1790, Pitt opposed, but in a half-hearted way, a motion for leave to bring in the Test and Corporation Acts.
  (b) In 1792, opposed a measure supported by Fox to repeal certain penal statutes against Unitarians.
  (c) Pitt's influence obtained the passage by the Irish Parliament of certain measures for the relief of the Catholics of Ireland.
  (d) After the union of England and Ireland, Pitt was of opinion that Roman Catholics might safely be admitted to office, and to the privilege of sitting in Parliament. As stated above, the king opposed the proposal, and Pitt resigned.

TWELFTH TOPIC.

THE CAREERS OF BURKE AND FOX.

(See articles in Encyclopædia Britannica.)

I. **Burke.** — "One of the greatest names in the history of political literature."

1. Born 1729 at Dublin, educated at Trinity College, Dublin, went to London 1750 to study law. Little known of this period of his life.
2. Made his first mark as writer by a satirical work, "A Vindication of Natural Society." Then followed his work "On the Sublime and Beautiful." Both works were published 1756. "By 1756 the cast of Burke's opinions were decisively fixed, and they underwent no radical change."

3. Began his public career in the service of "single speech" Hamilton, when the latter was Irish Secretary. In 1765 became private secretary to the Marquis of Rockingham, and in the following year was returned to Parliament for a pocket borough. "For the space of a quarter of a century, from this time down to 1790, Burke was one of the chief guides and inspirers of a revived Whig party." The policy of that party was opposition to the king's attempt at personal rule. Burke made speeches, and wrote books full of unanswerable arguments; but, all the same, the Commons voted for the king.
4. During these years Burke was a member of the club of which Reynolds and Garrick, Goldsmith and Johnson, were leading lights.
5. On the fall of the North Ministry, 1782, Burke was made paymaster of the forces, but held the office for only a few months. In 1783, he held the same position under the Coalition Ministry.
6. For fourteen years (1781-1795) he gave close attention to Indian affairs. The enormities of which Hastings was guilty aroused his indignation. His impeachment of Hastings was one of the interesting events in his career.
7. Burke distrusted the French Revolution from the first. When its excess revealed its true nature he determined to arouse the English nation against it. With this object he wrote "Reflections on the Revolution in France." Thirty thousand copies were sold within seven years. His views alienated him from his party. He sacrificed his friendship for Fox. He published an "Appeal from the New to the Old Whigs." Largely through his instrumentality, England was forced into war with France.
8. In 1794 Burke lost his son, in whom his hopes were wrapped up, and he never recovered from the blow.
9. Pitt's desire for peace called forth Burke's "Letters on a Regicide Peace." He died in the year following, the dark year of the war.

II. **Fox (1749-1806).**—" A statesman who, despite his failings, is one of the finest and most fascinating figures in modern history."

 1. Born in Westminster, educated at Eton and Oxford, travelled extensively in France and Italy, entered the House of Commons in 1768 for the pocket borough of Midhurst.
 2. Was third son of Henry Fox, "the most thoroughly hated statesman of his day"; was idolised by his father, but received from him a bad training. His father initiated him into gaming and other worse vices, and laughed at his son's scruples.
 3. At first supported the party of George III., and was made a Lord of the Admiralty; but, opposing the Royal Marriage Bill, incurred the displeasure of the king, and was never forgiven.
 4. "In 1774 Fox began that opposition to the ill-advised and ill-fated measures of Lord North which gave him a place among the greatest of orators and the most prominent of statesmen." Became a pupil of Burke's in political science, and was soon the acknowledged leader of the Opposition. The chief efforts of the Opposition at this time were directed against the king's policy in the American war.
 5. Became Secretary of State in the Marquis of Rockingham's administration, but held the position for a few months only. Became Secretary of State for a short time again in the coalition Ministry. The chief measures with which his name is associated are: (a) The treaties of peace between Great Britain and France, Spain, and the United States of America; (b) An India Bill.
 6. At the election of 1784 the whigs were left in a hopeless minority. Every effort was made to defeat Fox. His election was contested. In his subsequent parliamentary career he made many eloquent speeches, but accomplished little. The chief points in it are: (1) His opposition to Pitt's commercial treaty with France; (2) His opposition to the slave trade; (3) His attempts to have the Test and Corporation Acts repealed; (4) His support of a

thoroughgoing scheme of parliamentary reform; (5) His appointment as a manager in the impeachment of Warren Hastings; (6) His support of the claim of the Prince of Wales to be regent during his father's madness; (7) His Libel Act; (8) His friendly support of the French Revolution; (9) His opposition to the suspension of the Habeas Corpus Act, etc.; (10) His Support of the measures to resist Napoleon; (11) His appointment as Secretary of State, 1806; (12) His farewell speech against the slave trade.
7. Fox discontinued attendance in Parliament for some time (1797), and occupied himself with writing a History of England from James II.

THIRTEENTH TOPIC.

THE WAR WITH REVOLUTIONARY FRANCE (1793–1801).
I. Its Causes.

The spread of revolutionary principles on the continent excited the distrust of the conservative class in England. The excesses of the revolutionists aroused horror in all classes. Burke worked upon the fears of the English people until a panic of terror was excited. Pitt withstood the demand for war as long as he could, but in 1792 the French Convention decreed that France offer the aid of her soldiers to all nations who would strive for freedom. Further, in February, 1793, the French, having overrun Holland and conquered Flanders, threw open the navigation of the Scheldt, in violation of the Peace of Westphalia, and when the English envoy remonstrated he was ordered to quit the country, and war was declared against England.

II. Its Course.
1. Austria and Prussia attacked France on the north and east, Spain and Sardinia to the south, England kept the sea, and the peasantry of La Vendée rose in insurrection.

2. The war was at first disastrous to the French. They failed in their attack upon Holland, and were driven from the Netherlands. But the German powers were not anxious to restore order in France, as they wished to carry out their designs on Poland.
3. Soon an enthusiasm to spread liberty everywhere was awakened in France, and then her arms began to conquer wherever they went. An English force under the Duke of York, acting in the Netherlands, was so wasted by disease and hardship that it re-embarked for England. Lord Howe defeated the French fleet off Brest on the 1st June, 1794.
4. The year 1795 saw the coalition against France break up. Austria was the only ally of consequence England had, and she had to be heavily subsidized. Most of the French and Dutch colonial possessions fell into English hands.
5. In 1796 Pitt, heartily sick of the war, strove to bring about a peace, but the successes of Bonaparte in Italy led the French Government—the Directory—to decline all overtures. Spain entered into a treaty offensive and defensive with the French, and war was declared against Britain in October. The Spanish and Dutch fleets were now at the service of France. A French army under General Hoche set sail for Ireland in December, but the fleet was dispersed by a violent tempest and returned to France.
6. The year 1797 is the dark year of the war. Napoleon drove the Austrians completely out of Italy, and Austria was compelled to sign the Treaty of Campo Formio. England was left without an ally on the Continent. Her fleet mutinied—specie payments were suspended at the bank—Ireland was only waiting for an opportunity to revolt. Still she remained mistress of the sea. In February, Admiral Jervis defeated the Spanish fleet off Cape St. Vincent. In October, Admiral Duncan defeated the Dutch fleet off Camperdown.
7. In 1798 the Irish Catholics rose in arms. The insurgents were defeated at Vinegar Hill. Later in the year the

French General Humbert landed with 900 men; surrendered to Lord Cornwallis. In May of the same year Napoleon sailed for Egypt, his ultimate destination being India. He took Malta on the way, and arrived in Egypt, defeated the Mamelukes. Pushing into Syria, he was worsted at the siege of Acre (May, 1799) and compelled to retreat. Meantime (August, 1798) Nelson had annihilated the French fleet in Aboukir Bay. On the continent of Europe Russia joined with Austria to resist France, and Pitt encouraged the alliance by giving large subsidies.

8. The efforts of this coalition were successful in the beginning of 1799. French were defeated in Italy, but held their own in Switzerland and Holland. Napoleon returned from Egypt and was made First Consul. Russia retired from the coalition.

9. In the spring of 1800 Napoleon crossed the Alps at the St. Bernard, and defeated the Austrians at Marengo. Moreau also defeated them later in the year at Hohenlinden. Austria gladly made peace at Luneville, February, 1801.

10. In 1801 England was once more alone in opposition to France. Napoleon resolved to strike at England's commerce by shutting all European ports against her. He succeeded in uniting Russia, Sweden, and Denmark in an armed neutrality. The English fleet destroyed that of Denmark in the Battle of Copenhagen. A short time before this battle the Emperor Paul of Russia was assassinated, and his successor, Alexander, made a convention with England. Malta surrendered to the English, and the French army in Egypt capitulated.

11. Napoleon now resolved on peace for a time. PEACE OF AMIENS, March, 1802.

III. Conditions of Peace.

1. France to withdraw from Southern Italy, and to leave the Republics of Holland, Switzerland, and Piedmont to themselves.

2. England to recognize the French Government, to give back the captured colonies, except Ceylon and Trinidad, to restore Malta, within three months, to the knights of St. John.

FOURTEENTH TOPIC.

THE WAR WITH NAPOLEON.

I. **Its Cause.**

Napoleon resolute to become master of the Western World. Despite the pledge in the Peace of Amiens, the Republics of Holland, etc., made dependent upon his will. The protests of the English Government met by a demand that the French exiles be driven from England, and that Malta be surrendered. Huge armaments made ready for the invasion of England. War declared by England, May, 1803.

2. **Its Course to the beginning of the Peninsular War.**
   1. Napoleon formed a camp of 100,000 men at Boulogne, and sought to divide the English fleet, and to concentrate that of France, in order to cross the channel. The death of the French admiral prevented the plan from being carried out, and the assumption of the title of Emperor, and the ceremonies connected with his coronation, kept Napoleon engaged to the close of 1804.
   2. In 1805 Napoleon planned the union of the Spanish fleet with the French. Nelson was too quick for the French Admiral. The French and Spanish navies were annihilated off Cape Trafalgar, 21st October. Meanwhile a league of Russia, Austria, and Sweden was formed against Napoleon. Pitt gave subsidies. Napoleon, disappointed in his plans against England, marched his army against the Austrians and Russians. He crushed their combined forces at Austerlitz, 2nd December. Results: (1) The Treaty of Presburg, by which Austria

ceded all her Italian and Adriatic Provinces; (2) The
dissolution of the old German Empire.
3. In October, 1806, Prussia was crushed at Jena. In November Napoleon issued his "Berlin Decrees."
4. In January, 1807, the English Government replied by an
"Order-in-Council," declaring France and allied countries blockaded, and neutral vessels trading with them
good prizes. In June, 1807, Napoleon defeated the Russians
at Friedland. Battle was followed by the Peace of Tilsit.
Russia became friendly to France, and forced Sweden to
renounce her alliance with England. The Russian and
Swedish fleets were put at the service of France, and
Napoleon counted on that of Denmark also. In September an English fleet bombarded Copenhagen, and seized
the Danish fleet. In November England issued fresh
Orders-in-Council, bearing still more heavily on neutrals.
In December Napoleon issued in return his Milan
Decree.

3. The Peninsular War.

A. How it came to be entered upon.

Napoleon was seeking to unite all Europe against England: in particular, he wished to close the continent against English goods. Spain had been the subservient ally of France for some years, but Napoleon wanted to have full control of the country. He forced the King to resign, and appointed his brother Joseph to the vacant throne. The Spaniards refused to acknowledge him. The English Government gladly offered to support them.

B. Its Course.

1. Sir John Moore and Sir Arthur Wellesley were sent with small armies, 1808. Wellesley gained the battle of Vimiera, and forced a French army to surrender in Convention of Cintra.

Sir John Moore advanced into Spain, found himself opposed by forces much larger than his own, and made a masterly retreat of 250 miles to the coast. Was killed in the battle of CORUNNA, January, 1809.

2. French troops were sent (1809) to Wellesley, to 1st again Hernanded the Douro, compelled Soult to retreat; then marching on Madrid, defeated a French army at TALAVERA (July). Had to retreat on Badajos, and to allow Ciudad Rodrigo and Almeida to be captured. Checked the advance of Massena at BUSACO, but fell back on TORRES VEDRAS, October, 1810.

3. Massena was compelled to retreat, and Wellington followed and besieged Almeida. Battles of FUENTES D'ONORE, May, 1811. Portugal was saved from the French, but Spain was in their hands.

4. Napoleon withdrew the best of his troops from Spain, and Wellington assumed the offensive, 1812. CIUDAD RODRIGO and BADAJOS were captured. Wellington marched on SALAMANCA, defeated Marmont (July 22nd), and in August entered Madrid. Besieged Burgos—but the approach of two French armies compelled a retreat to the frontiers of Portugal (October).

5. In May, 1813, Wellington again advanced from Portugal, defeated the French at VITTORIA, and drove them across the Pyrenees. In July he carried SAN SEBASTIAN by assault. Gained the battle of Bidassoa in October, which enabled him to enter Spain (1814). Drove Soult from an entrenched camp at Bayonne, and defeated him at Orthes. In April, an indecisive battle fought at Toulouse—the last of the war.

IV. **The War in Europe from 1808 to the Battle of Waterloo.**

1. In September, 1808, Napoleon went into an intimate alliance with the Czar of Russia, in order to prevent the German powers from renewing hostilities.
2. In 1809 Austria determined once more to renew the struggle with Napoleon. Battles of Wagram, July 5th and 6th. An English force sent against Antwerp, returned after heavy losses.
3. In 1810 Napoleon dispossessed his brother Louis of the kingdom of Holland, on account of his laxity in carrying

out the continental system, and added the country to France. He also sought an alliance with the United States against Britain.

4. "In February, 1811, the United States announced that all intercourse with Great Britain and her dependencies was at an end"—a serious blow to English commerce. Besides this, Napoleon seized several States, among others the duchy of Oldenburg, for trading with England. The Duke of Oldenburg was a brother-in-law of Czar Alexander, and the latter resented Napoleon's action. He resolved to disregard the continental blockade of British manufactures. Napoleon determined to punish him.

5. In May, 1812, Napoleon set out from Paris to superintend the invasion of Russia. In June the United States declared war against England.

6. In the spring of 1813 Prussia rose in arms against Napoleon. Later in the year Austria, stirred to action by the successes of Wellington, joined Prussia and Russia. Napoleon was defeated by the allied forces at Leipzig in October. On the last day of 1813, the allies entered France.

7. In March, 1814, the allies entered Paris. On April 4th Napoleon abdicated and was sent to Elba. The TREATY OF PARIS closed the war. The TREATY OF GHENT concluded the war with America.

8. On the 1st of March, 1815, Napoleon landed at Cannes, and in twenty days he was in Paris. On June 18th he met Wellington at Waterloo and was defeated.

FIFTEENTH TOPIC.

THE SOCIAL CONDITION OF ENGLAND IN THE EIGHTEENTH CENTURY.

(Knight's History of England may be consulted with advantage.)

IV. Increase of Population.

From 1700 to 1750, 200,000; from 1750 to 1780, nearly a million and a quarter; from 1780 to 1801, nearly a million and a half. "The start in the national industry, supplying new sources of profitable labor and the means of subsistence to increasing numbers, appears to have been singularly concurrent with that outburst of public spirit which attended the administration of the first William Pitt."—*Knight.*

II. **Morals and Manners of the People.**
  1. The manners of the upper classes were refined, their morals loose. Walpole sneered at all appeals to patriotism or any of the higher feelings. The Duke of Grafton appeared in public with his mistress. Fox was a gambler.
  2. The middle classes were the salt of the country—God-fearing, intelligent, law-abiding.
  3. The common people were sunk in terrible ignorance and brutality. The Methodist revival did them untold good
  4. "In Walpole's day the English clergy were the idlest and the most lifeless in the world." The Methodist revival made the fox-hunting parson and the absentee rector impossible

III. **Religious Progress.**
  1. In the early part of the century among the upper classes Deism prevailed extensively. Christianity was regarded as an exploded belief.
  2. The Methodist revival was confined almost entirely to the lower and middle classes. Whitfield, the orator; John Wesley, the organizer; Charles Wesley, the poet of the movement.
  3. The reflex influence of the movement on the Established Church very great. It created an evangelical party within the Church.
  4. The noblest fruits of the revival were: (*a*) The new moral enthusiasm; (*b*) the new philanthropy. Hence: (1) Prison Reform (note career of Howard); (2) Repeal of Penal Laws; (3) Abolition of Slave Trade; (4) The beginning of popular Education.

IV. Progress in Manufactures.

1. In 1770 one man in three was engaged in agriculture; in 1850, one man in four. The great advancement in the mechanical arts began just at the accession of George III.
2. The names of the great inventors and discoverers of the end of last century are Brindley, Arkwright, Crompton, Cartwright, Roebuck, Wedgewood, Watt.
3. The first canals were opened in the first years of George III.'s reign. The coal trade at once sprang up. Arkwright took out a patent for a spinning machine, 1769. Mobs burned the mills in which they were used. Crompton's "mule" was finished 1779. Steam power was first employed in spinning, 1787. Cartwright's power-loom was first brought into profitable use in 1801.
4. Dr. John Roebuck's name is connected with two important inventions: (1) A process for producing sulphuric acid cheap; (2) the process of smelting iron (1759).
5. In 1793 Wedgewood produced a new kind of earthenware that soon drove out the wooden and pewter dishes.
6. In 1774 Watt's first steam engine was set up in Birmingham.

SIXTEENTH TOPIC.

LITERATURE AND ART IN THE EIGHTEENTH CENTURY.

(Refer to Chambers' Cyclopædia of Literature.)

I. Literature.
A. Poets.

During this period there is a gradual transition from the classical school of Pope to the natural school of the beginning of the present century.

1. Edward Young (1681-1765).—Night Thoughts.
2. James Thomson (1700-1748).—The Seasons.
3. William Collins (1721-1759).—Ode to Liberty, etc.

4. Thomas Gray (1716-1771).—Elegy in a Country Churchyard.
5. Oliver Goldsmith (1728-1774).—The Deserted Village.
6. William Cowper (1731-1800).—The Task.
7. Robert Burns (1759-1796).—The Cottar's Saturday Night
8. William Wordsworth (1770-1850).—The Excursion.
9. Samuel Taylor Coleridge (1772-1834.—The Ancient Mariner.
10. Sir Walter Scott (1771-1832).—Lay of the Last Minstrel.
11. Thomas Moore (1779-1852).—Irish Melodies.
12. Lord Byron (1788-1824).—Childe Harold.
13. Percy Bysshe Shelley (1792-1822).—Revolt of Islam.
14. John Keats (1795-1820).—Endymion.

B. Novelists.
1. Samuel Richardson (1689-1761).—Clarissa Harlowe.
2. Henry Fielding (1707-1754).—Tom Jones.
3. Tobias Smollett (1721-1771).—Roderick Random.
4. Dr. Samuel Johnson (1709-1784).—Rasselas.
5. Sir Walter Scott.—Waverly.

C. Historians.
1. Tobias Smollett.—History of England.
2. David Hume (1711-1776).—History of England.
3. Dr. William Robertson (1721-1793).—History of Scotland.
4. Edward Gibbon (1737-1794).—Decline and Fall of the Roman Empire.

D. Metaphysicians.
1. David Hume.—Treatise on Human Nature.
2. Dr. Adam Smith (1723-1790).—Theory of Moral Sentiments.
3. Dr. Thomas Reid (1710-1796).—The Intellectual Powers of Man.
4. Dr. Dugald Stewart (1753-1828).—Philosophy of the Human Mind.

E. Theologians.
1. Dr. Joseph Butler (1692-1752).—Analogy of Religion to the Course of Nature.

2. John Wesley (1703-1791).—Sermons.
3. George Whitfield (1714-1770).—Sermons.
4. Dr. William Paley (1743-1805).—Natural Theology.

F. **Essayists.**
1. Dr. Samuel Johnson.—The Rambler and The Idler.
2. Dr. Hawkesworth.—The Adventurer.
3. Horace Walpole. ⎫
4. Earl of Chesterfield and others. ⎬ The World.
5. Rev. Sydney Smith. ⎫
6. Francis Jeffrey. ⎬ Edinburgh Review.
7. Lord Brougham. ⎭

G. **Dramatists.**
1. David Garrick (1716-1779).—The Lying Valet.
2. Samuel Foote.—The Minor.
3. Oliver Goldsmith.—She Stoops to Conquer.
4. Richard Brinsley Sheridan.—The Rivals.
5. George Colman.—John Bull.

II. Art.
1. HOGARTH.—" The true founder of the English School of Painting."
2. REYNOLDS.—" The acknowledged leader in portraiture."
3. GAINSBOROUGH.—"A painter both of landscape and portrait in a style at once thoroughly English and thoroughly original."
4. Wilson.—He was a great painter, but his painting was conventional."
5. West.—Painted "Death of General Wolfe."
6. Lawrence.—" The undisputed successor to Reynolds."
7. Wilkie.—Painter of the " pleasant side of every-day life."
8. Turner.—" His 'Crossing the Brook' is the noblest English landscape of its kind ever painted."

THE ROYAL ACADEMY was founded in 1768.—" The list of original members is a curious index to the state of art in England at that time. Of the thirty-three whose names are inserted in the first catalogue, eight or nine are foreigners; two are ladies; some were coach and sign painters—most are mere sorry men; probably not more than half a dozen would be recognised enough to the students of the literature of art."

III. Sculpture.
   1. Banks (reign of George III.).—The first great English sculptor.
   2. Bacon (John) designed a very large proportion of the public monuments of England at the end of last century.
   3. Flaxman. - "Some of his grander productions, like the Archangel Michael and Satan, are the glory of the English school of sculpture."

IV. Architecture.
   1. Sir Robert Taylor, the leading architect when George III. came to the throne.
   2. Sir John Soane.—Architect to the Bank of England.
   3. Sir William Chambers.—Architect of "Somerset House."

SEVENTEENTH TOPIC.

THE HOUSE OF LORDS SINCE THE REVOLUTION.
(See May in particular.)

1. The influence of the House of Lords very great, but gradually becoming less.
2. Its increase in numbers. At beginning of Henry VII.'s reign only 29 temporal peers; at death of Elizabeth, 59; at Revolution, 150; at accession of George III., 174. Between 1700 and 1821, 667 were created, of which 388 were created between 1761 and 1821.
3. Character of this increase. The House of Lords "is no longer a council of the magnates of the land - the territorial aristocracy, the descendants or representatives of the barons of the olden time." The additions to the peerage have consisted of eminent men in various walks of life.

4. The principle of representation in the House of Lords:
   (a) There are 28 peers of Ireland elected for life.
   (b) Scottish peerage, represented by 16 peers, elected for a single Parliament only,
   (c) English spiritual peers number 28, holding seats for life.
5. Importance of the prerogative of creating peers:
   (a) Attempts made in 1719 to fix the number of peers. Defeated chiefly through the exertions of Walpole.
   (b) Power to create peers prevents a dead-lock between Commons and Lords.
   (c) Creation of peers in House of Lords equivalent to a dissolution in the Commons.

EIGHTEENTH TOPIC.

THE HOUSE OF COMMONS SINCE THE REVOLUTION.

(See May in particular.)

I. **Number of Members.**
   1. Under the last two Stuarts average number of members 500.
   2. Union with Scotland added 45.
   3. Union with Ireland added 100.
   4. Number since averaged about 650. House which met January, 1886, had 670 members.

II. **As Representative of the People.**
   1. Defects of the system of representation previous to 1832:
      (a) Nomination boroughs.
      (b) Partial and uncertain rights of election.
      (c) Flagrant bribery at elections.
      (d) Seats bought and sold.
      (e) Government influence in large towns.
      (f) Cost of elections in the great cities.
      (g) Many large towns unrepresented.

2. Some examples of the defects.
   (a) "Seventy members were returned by thirty-six places in which there were scarcely any electors at all." "The Duke of Norfolk was represented by eleven members; Lord Lonsdale by nine," etc.
   (b) At New Shoreham an association, "The Christian Club," was in the habit of selling the representation to the highest bidder, and after the election, distributing the money among its members.
   (c) Men who had amassed fortunes in the Indies (Nabobs) and whose careers had made them unscrupulous "forced their way into Parliament by such a torrent of corruption as no private hereditary fortune could resist." As much as £5,000 was given for a seat.
   (d) "The poll was liable to be kept open for forty days. . During this period the public houses were thrown open, and drunkenness and disorder prevailed in the streets and at the hustings. Bands of hired ruffians —armed with bludgeons and inflamed by drink— paraded the public thoroughfares, intimidating voters and resisting their access to the polling places."

3. Attempts to remedy these defects:—
   (a) Wilkes' scheme (1776) proposed to give additional members to London and the large counties, to disfranchise the rotten boroughs, and to enfranchise Manchester, Leeds, etc.
   (b) Duke of Richmond (1780) proposed annual parliaments, universal suffrage, and equal electoral districts.
   (c) Mr. Pitt moved several motions for reform (1782 1785). Proposed (1785) "that seventy-two members, then returned by thirty-six decayed boroughs, should be distributed among the counties and the metropolis." Compensation was to be given to the proprietors. Some thirty other seats were to be purchased and distributed. The king thoroughly opposed the scheme.

(d) "The matter was now allowed to drop, and the terror caused by the outbreak of the French Revolution some years later rendered all efforts at reform useless."

The Reform Bill of 1832, introduced by Lord John Russell, provided :—

1. That the franchise should be taken from fifty-six "rotten boroughs."
2. That one hundred and forty-three large towns or counties without representation should have the right to elect members.
3. That householders paying £10 rental should be allowed to vote in boroughs.
4. That leaseholders should have the franchise in counties.

III. The History of Parties since the Revolution.

1. Under William and Anne the two great parties, Whigs and Tories, about equally balanced. Whigs inclined to limit the royal power, Tories to extend it. Whigs in favor of religious toleration, Tories against it. Whigs favorable to the House of Hanover, Tories inclined to recall the Stuarts. Whigs mostly merchants and manufacturers, Tories mostly clergymen and land owners.
2. During the reign of George I. and George II., the Tory party was gone.
3. After the overthrow of the Stuart cause in 1745, the Tories became a national party. They rally round George III., become "the King's Friends."
4. The Whig party broken up into factions by the jealousies of rival families, and the intriguing of the king.
5. The Tories support the king in his efforts to chastise the American colonies. The Whigs, after in vain opposing the king's measures, secede from Parliament (1776). Return weaker than ever.
6. After fall of North and Rockingham ministries, there are three parties, Lord Shelburne and the Court Party ; Lord

North and his Tory adherents. Mr. Fox and the Whigs. The two last united against the first led by Pitt, the younger. After a prolonged struggle they were defeated. The Tories continue in the ascendant during the remainder of the period.

7. Effect of the French Revolution on the parties. The Whigs look on with sympathy, the Tories with indignation and alarm. Mr. Burke's views.

IV. Duration of Parliament.

1. In 1664 the Triennial Act of Charles I.'s reign was repealed, and provision made "that Parliament should not be interrupted above three years at the most." Effect: King might keep the Parliament sitting as long as he liked.
2. Bill of Rights declared that Parliament ought to be held frequently.
3. Triennial Act (1694) provided: (a) That a new Parliament should be called within three years after the dissolution of a former one; (b) No Parliament should sit longer than three years.
4. Septennial Act (1715) extended the period of duration to seven years.
5. In practice, Parliament seldom lasts seven years. Out of eleven Parliaments of George III. only eight lasted six.

V. Privileges of Parliament.

1. Right of expelling members:
    (a) Sir Richard Steele expelled (1714) for writing a pamphlet reflecting on the ministry of the day.
    (b) Wilkes' case. Imprisoned on a general warrant for reflecting on the king in No. 45 of the *North Briton*. Released on his privilege as an M.P. Whilst matter still before the courts, the House of Commons expel him. He retires to France for a time. Is re-elected (1768), and again expelled. Is again returned. House expels him, and declares that he is incapable of re-election. Again elected (by a majority of 847),

but his opponent permitted to take the seat. In 1774 Wilkes was again returned and permitted to take his seat. In 1782 the proceedings against him were expunged from the records of the Commons "as being subversive of the rights of the whole body of the electors of the kingdom."—*T-L.*

2. Right of committing to prison. Extends only to the duration of the session of Parliament. See Murray's case in *T-L.*

3. Publication of Debates:
   (a) After the Revolution, frequent resolutions passed to prevent the publication of debates—without avail.
   (b) Imperfect reports appeared from time to time in Magazines, sometimes as the proceedings of the "Senate of Great Lilliput," etc.
   (c) Notes had to be taken by stealth; reports generally inaccurate. Dr. Johnson "took care that the Whig dogs should not have the best of it."
   (d) Reports of speeches accompanied with the names of the speakers first appeared 1771. Col. Onslow complains of some of these reports.
   (e) Commons order printers to appear at the bar. Wilkes arranges a scheme by which the House is brought into conflict with the Corporation of London. The Lord Mayor committed to prison.
   (f) Publication of debates since pursued without any restraint.
   (g) The privilege of reporting may be withdrawn at any time.

4. Right of Commons to levy taxes and vote supplies:
   (a) This right freely acknowledged since the Revolution.
   (b) "Stopping the Supplies" only once attempted (1784) since the Revolution.
   (c) Lords can only assent to the appropriation bills.

5. Reform Bills since 1832
   (a) Lord Derby's bill of 1867 gave the franchise to all ratepayers in boroughs, to all lodgers in boroughs

...occupying farms rented at £10 a year, and he had lands besides in .... It took 50 members from English boroughs and gave 25 seats to English counties, and the other eight to Ireland and Scotland.

(b) In 1872 the system of voting secretly by ballot was adopted.

(c) In 1885 the franchise was extended by Mr. Gladstone to include agricultural labourers.

NINETEENTH TOPIC.

THE PRESS AND LIBERTY OF OPINION.
(See May, Chap. IX.)

1. Under the Stuarts political discussion was suppressed with barbarous severity. Milton's Areopagitica was a plea for Unlicensed Printing. The Licensing Act of the reign of Charles II. placed the entire control of printing in the Government. The Act, after being several times renewed, was allowed to expire 1695, and from that date "a censorship of the press was for ever renounced by the law of England."

2. The restraint henceforth upon the freedom of the press was the law of libel. This law harshly administered.

3. Newspapers assumed their present form in Queen Anne's reign. The political writings of that time so "ferocious" that a new restraint—a stamp duty—was imposed in 1712. The great writers of this period—Addison, Steele, Swift, Bolingbroke.

4. No marked advance in the next two reigns. "Writers were hired by statesmen to decry the measures and blacken the characters of their rivals; and, instead of seeking to instruct the people, devoted their talents to the personal service of their employers, and the narrowest interests of faction.

5. The Government of George III. soon fell foul of the press. It had been the custom of journalists to refer to public men under cover of their initials; the "North Briton," Wilkes' paper, assailed them openly by name. No. 45 of that paper attacked the king and Bute. The Government resolved to prosecute. A "General Warrant" was issued to discover the authors and publishers; on a question of privilege Wilkes was excluded from Parliament; and, lastly, Wilkes was prosecuted in the Court of King's Bench. Public sympathy was aroused for Wilkes, and popular riots took place.

6. Before the excitement over Wilkes' case had died out the letters of Junius appeared. In the trial springing out of this case two doctrines were asserted: (1) That a publisher was criminally liable for the acts of his servants; (2) That the publication of a libel by a publisher's servant was proof of his criminality. A third doctrine was asserted by Lord Mansfield, that the judge alone must decide on the criminality of the libel.

7. Mr. Erskine won great fame in opposing these doctrines. In face of the opposition of the most renowned judges of the day, Mr. Foxe's Libel Act was passed 1792. It gave to the juries the right to decide the criminality of the libel.

8. The excitement of the French Revolution caused the publication of many seditious opinions. Thomas Payne was tried for using seditious language in his "Rights of Man"; was defended by Mr. Erskine. Paine was found guilty. The Government adopted a repressive policy 1792. Many trials took place for using seditious language, and so great was the panic, that a verdict of guilty was generally returned. Of the twenty-eight years that follow, May says: "The last twenty-eight years of the reign of George III., formed a period of perilous transition for liberty of opinion. While the right of free discussion had been discredited by factious license, by wild and dangerous theories, by turbulence and sedition—the Government and Legislature, in guarding against these excesses, had discountenanced and

ppressed legitimate agitation. . . . Authority was placed in constant antagonism to large masses of the people, who had no voice in the government of their country. Mutual distrust and alienation grew up between them. The people lost confidence in rulers whom they knew only by oppressive taxes, and harsh laws severely administered. The Government, harassed by suspicions of disaffection, detected conspiracy and treason in every murmur of popular discontent."

TWENTIETH TOPIC.

RELIGIOUS LIBERTY.

1. Religious Toleration is one of the latest developments of national life. The early idea was that the Church and the nation were coterminous, and that any one separating from the Church, put himself outside the protection of the nation.

2. The efforts to crush out dissent during the Stuart period failed. At the Revolution Dissenters rendered important services. Hence the Toleration Act. Its provisions:
   (a) It exempted from the penalties of existing statutes against separate conventicles, and absence from church, all persons who should take the oaths of allegiance and supremacy, and subscribe a declaration against transubstantiation.
   (b) It relieved the dissenting ministers from the restrictions imposed by the Act of Uniformity and the Conventicle Act, on condition that, in addition to taking the oaths, they signed the 39 Articles, with certain exceptions.
   (c) It allowed Quakers to affirm instead of taking the oaths.
   (d) It required all "meeting-houses" to be registered.
   (e) It specially excepted Roman Catholics and Unitarians from the Act.

3. Penal laws against Roman Catholics were passed from time to time. An Act passed in 1700 enacted:
   (a) That a reward of £100 be given for the discovery of a Roman Catholic priest exercising his functions.
   (b) That a priest so found be imprisoned for life.
   (c) That a Roman Catholic could not inherit or purchase land unless he abjured his religion upon oath.
   (d) That he could not send his children abroad to be educated.
4. An inroad upon the Toleration Act was made by an Act (1711) against occasional conformity, and another (1713) to prevent the growth of schism. Both these were repealed in the following reign.
5. The relaxation of the Penal Code followed upon the religious revival of the middle of the century.
6. A Roman Catholic Relief Act was passed 1778 without a dissentient voice. It repealed the Penal Statute of 1700.
7. The Test and Corporation Acts were repealed 1828.
8. Next year (1829) the Catholic Emancipation Act was passed.
9. Jews were admitted to Parliament for the first time in 1845.

TWENTY-FIRST TOPIC.

THE GREAT STATESMEN OF THE NINETEENTH CENTURY.

(NOTE—For Pitt, see Eleventh Topic.)

1. **Canning.**—After Pitt, by far the most brilliant statesman of England in the first quarter of the century was Canning. He was an admirer of Pitt, and endeavored to carry out Pitt's policy of encouraging commercial progress at home, but he was more decided in his foreign policy.

   His best work was done as Secretary of Foreign Affairs, 1807-1809 and 1822-1827. During his first term as Foreign Secretary he proved the ablest opponent of Napoleon, and in his second term he undid the mischief of the Holy Alliance, and extended England's influence in Foreign affairs. He revived Pitt's agitation in favor of the removal of Catholic disabilities. He became First Lord of the Treasury in 1827, but died four months after the formation of his ministry.

2. **Lord Grey and Lord Melburne.**—From 1830 to 1840 England was guided chiefly by these two statesmen. They were by no means so brilliant as many other statesmen of the century, but they passed some of the most important legislation ever enacted in England. Their chief acts were:—

   (a) The Reform Bill of 1832.
   (b) The suppression of the Slave Trade, 1833.
   (c) The new Poor Law of 1834.
   (d) The Municipal Act of 1835, restoring the right of self-government to towns.
   (e) The encouragement of national education by government grants from 1834, and by establishing an Educational Committee of the Privy Council in 1839.

3. **Peel.**—Judged by the number of statues erected to his memory, no statesman was ever more popular in England than Sir Robert Peel. He was, next to Canning, the ablest man in the House of Commons in the "twenties." On the death of Lord Liverpool he refused to serve under Canning, on account of Canning's liberality towards Roman Catholics. In 1828 he became leader of the Commons under Wellington, and passed the Catholic Emancipation Act in 1829. Wellington's ministry resigned in 1830, and Peel did not return to power for more than ten years, except for four months, 1834-1835. He was Prime Minister for five years. His greatest work was the repeal of the Corn Laws and the extension of British influence in India. The repeal of the Corn Laws gave great offence to his own party, and he was forced to resign in 1846.

4. **Lord John Russell** was a prominent leader for forty years. He introduced the Reform Bill of 1832, and on the retirement of Peel in 1846 he became Prime Minister, and remained in

power for six years. He was again Prime Minister in 1865, but was defeated on a second Reform Bill, and retired in 1866.

5. **Lord Palmerston** was the guiding statesman of the empire for ten years from 1855 to 1865, with the exception of a few months in 1858-9. He was a very able man, whose policy was inaction at home and the avoidance of complications abroad. The Crimean War came to him as a legacy. He prosecuted it to a successful issue, and showed vigor and statesmanship in quelling the revolt in India in 1857. He transferred the sovereignty of India from the East India Company to the Crown in 1858. The volunteer movement developed during his rule. He was successful in avoiding all foreign wars during the last six years of his term of office, and did much to bring about England's polity of peace and the settlement of international disputes by arbitration.

6. **Disraeli and Gladstone.**—Since Lord Palmerston's death in 1865 these two statesmen have been the great leaders of the English people. Mr. Disraeli introduced the Reform Bill of 1867, and became one of the most successful political leaders of the century. Mr. Gladstone, who began life as a Conservative, became the leader of the Liberals, and passed a number of progressive measures of great importance. Among them are:—

    (*a*) The Disestablishment of the Irish Church in 1869.

    (*b*) The establishing of School Boards and providing for their support by local rates, 1870.

    (*c*) The abolition of religious tests in Universities, 1871.

    (*d*) The introduction of the secret ballot in elections, 1872.

    (*e*) The Franchise Act of 1885, giving the right to vote to agricultural laborers.

TWENTY-SECOND TOPIC.

PRIME MINISTERS FROM 1763 TO THE PRESENT TIME.

Mr. George Grenville	April 1763 to	June 1765
Marquess of Rockingham	July 1765 "	July 1766
Pitt, Earl of Chatham	July 1766 "	Oct. 1768
Duke of Grafton	Oct. 1768 "	Jan. 1770
Lord North	Jan. 1770 "	Mar. 1782
Marquess of Rockingham	Mar. 1782 "	July 1782
Earl of Shelburne	July 1782 "	Feb. 1783
Duke of Portland (Coalition Ministry) ..	April 1783 "	Dec. 1783
Mr. William Pitt (the younger)	Dec. 1783 "	Feb. 1801
Mr. Addington	Feb. 1801 "	April 1804
Mr. William Pitt	May 1804 "	Jan. 1806
Lord Grenville (Ministry of all the Talents	Feb. 1806 "	Mar. 1807
Duke of Portland	Mar. 1807 "	Oct. 1810
Mr. Spencer Perceval	Oct. 1810 "	May 1812
Lord Liverpool	May 1812 "	April 1827
Mr. George Canning	April 1827 "	Aug. 1827
Lord Goderich	Aug. 1827 "	Jan. 1828
Duke of Wellington	Jan. 1828 "	Nov. 1830
Lord Grey	Nov. 1830 "	July 1834
Lord Melbourne	April 1835 "	Aug. 1841
Sir Robert Peel	Aug. 1841 "	July 1846
Lord John Russell	July 1846 "	Feb. 1852
Lord Derby	Feb. 1852 "	Dec. 1852
Lord Aberdeen	Dec. 1852 "	Feb. 1855
Lord Palmerston	Feb. 1855 "	Feb. 1858

Lord Derby	Feb. 1858 "	June 1859
Lord Palmerston	June 1859 "	Nov. 1865
Earl Russsll	Nov. 1865 "	June 1866
Lord Derby	June 1866 "	Feb. 1868
Mr. Disraeli	Feb. 1868 "	Dec. 1868
Mr. Gladstone	Dec. 1868 "	Feb. 1874
Mr. Disraeli	Feb. 1874 "	April 1880
Mr. Gladstone	April 1880 "	June 1885
Lord Salisbury	June 1885 "	Feb. 1886
Mr. Gladstone	Feb. 1886 "	Aug. 1886
Lord Salisbury	Aug. 1886 "	Aug. 1892
Mr. Gladstone	Aug. 1892 "	Mar. 1894
Lord Roseberry	Mar. 1894 "	June 1895
Lord Salisbury	June 1895	

FRANCE AFTER THE TREATY OF 1359.
(The dotted line encloses the lands held by the King of England.)

FRANCE AFTER THE PEACE OF BRETIGNY.

(The dotted lines enclose the Dominions of the King of England.)

A TOPICAL ANALYSIS
OF
GREEK HISTORY.

FIRST TOPIC.

THE LEGENDARY PERIOD.

1. The chief sources of the Greek Legends or Myths are the writings of Orpheus, Hesiod and Homer.

2. The earliest known inhabitants of Greece were the Pelasgi who are believed to be an Asiatic tribe.

> "Tradition and etymology agree in tracing the Pelasgians, or back to the western and northern coast of Asia Minor. There is, however, little or no reason to doubt that the bulk of the race, on a track these 'swarthy Asiatics' belonged, entered Europe for the first time through the wide district of Thrace, which is also considered to be the most ancient European settlement of this tribe."—*Jerusalem.*

> "If any man is inclined to call the undiscovered ages of Greece by the name of Pelasgic, it appears to him no doubt that term to be a name carrying with it no admitted predicates, neither enlivening an insight into real history, nor enabling us to explain—what would be the real historical problem—how or from whom the Hellenes acquired that stock of dispositions, aptitudes, arts, &c., with which they enter on their career."—*Grote.*

3. The Hellenes.

   1. From a small tribe in northern Thessaly came the original Hellenes. It is claimed by some that they were of Pelasgic stock, but Niebuhr ridicules this theory. The name Hellenes came to be applied to the Greek people and ultimately included those Greeks who were of Pelasgic origin.

   > "Both metropolitans and colonists styled themselves Hellenes, and were recognized as such by each other; all as to refer to the common of its prominent symbol of fraternity—all describing non-Hellenic races of cities by a word which involved sentiments of repugnance."—*Nöt.*

4. The Hellenes were divided into three leading branches: Ionians, Æolians, and Dorians.

5. **Foreign Immigrations.**
   1. Cecrops, about 1555 B.C., came with a colony from Egypt and settled in Attica. The legend states that he founded Athens, and that he first called it Cecropia, afterwards changed to Athena after the goddess of his tribe. Hermann states that the legend of the Egyptian colonization of Attica was never acknowledged by the Athenians themselves.
   2. Cadmus about 1550 B.C. came from Phœnicia and settled in Bœotia. He founded Thebes, and introduced letters into Greece, and also music and the arts of working in metals.

      "A division of them, under the name of Cadmeians, occupied Bœotia, and either driving out the natives, or uniting with them, founded there the celebrated city of Thebes. Cadmus, the leader of this colony, has the fame of introducing letters into Greece; but the merit of this, and all the improvements which took place at the same period, belongs to him only in common with the other chiefs of the Curetes."—*Grote.*

   3. Pelops, 1283 B.C., came from Phrygia and settled in the Peloponnesus.

6. The greatest king of legendary times was Theseus, who was the tenth king of Athens. He lived about 1230 B.C. He united the twelve cities of Attica and contributed largely to the prosperity of the country.

7. The Trojan war is the most striking story of the history of legendary Greece. To it is attributed the kindling of a national spirit of unity among the Hellenic nations.

   "From the time of the Trojan war downwards, the Hellenes always looked upon themselves as but one people."—*Hermann.*

   The siege of Troy lasted ten years and ended in the destruction of Troy by the trick of the Wooden horse. The leading Greek heroes according to the Homeric legend were, Agamemnon, Menelaus, Nestor, Ajax and Achilles.

   "Though literally believed, reverentially cherished, and numbered among the gigantic phenomena of the past, by the Grecian public, the Trojan war is, in the eyes of modern inquiry, essentially a legend and nothing more."—*Grote.*

8. Dorian Conquest of the Peloponnesus.
1. This is generally called "The return of the Heraclidæ." The descendants of Heracles had been expelled by Pelops, and settled among the Dorians. They induced the Dorians finally to make common cause with them and succeeded in the conquest of all the Peloponnesus except Arcadia and Achaia. This important movement took place about 1100 B.C.

9. Great Authors of the Legendary Period.
Homer about 950 B.C., Hesiod a century later.

10. End of Kingly Rule in Athens.
Codrus last king 1045 B.C. No successor allowed, because the people thought no one worthy to succeed him. For nearly 300 years Athens was governed by Archons, who were practically kings and who ruled for life.

11. The great rival of Athens was Sparta, and before the close of the legendary period these two cities centred in themselves the whole of the elements of Grecian development.

SECOND TOPIC.

THE CONSTITUTIONS OF SPARTA AND ATHENS.

1. Lycurgus, the great Spartan law giver, really belongs to the mythical period. Two dates are given for the issue of his remarkable laws, 884 and 817 B.C. Sparta emerged from the legendary period with a definite system of laws, and with a profound reverence for their national constitution. Probably in no other country in the world was the character of an entire people so completely altered by its laws as in Sparta.

2. The main features of the Constitution were:
There were two kings descended from the Heraclidæ. They presided over the senate or council. The senate or council consisted of twenty-eight elders who held office for life. The kings had almost unlimited authority in time of war and

when away from Spartan territory. Both the kings and the senate were restrained by the Ephori, five magistrates chosen by the people by general vote. The Ephori held a controlling and somewhat peculiar position. They presided at general assemblies of the people and conducted all elections. They made war and peace, but they had to be unanimous before their decisions were binding. They ultimately assumed nearly all the functions of executive government. The Spartans themselves were forbidden to work in cultivation of the land or in manual labor. The workers were the Helots. Iron money was used. The whole people ate at public tables and the fare was simple and inexpensive. The aim of training was to develop physical strength and endurance, and a spirit of subordination of the individual to the state in all things. Even human life was regarded as belonging primarily to the state and not to the individual, and the natural affection of parents was to a large extent eradicated by the law that made men and women simple elements in the unity called the state, and led mothers to rejoice in the death of their sons if they died nobly for Sparta. The Spartan reverence for law was one of the greatest lessons Sparta gave to the other Greek states.

3. Athenian Lawgivers.

Draco, 621 B.C.

"Draco's enactments, B.C. 621, made no change in the constitution, unless it were that the substitution of definite penalties for the previously arbitrary sentence of the archons gave rise to the court of appeal of the Ephetæ."—*Hermann*.

"The precise nature of the institutions of Draco, though they have become proverbial for their sanguinary character, is little known. He renewed an extravagant law for the prosecution even of inanimate things which had caused the death of anyone. Another law, attributed to him by Diogenes Laertius, was designed for the prevention of idleness; a habit which was differently estimated at Sparta, where it formed a distinction between the free citizen and the slave."—*Ottman*.

The laws of Draco were very severe. They were principally a criminal code in which the universal punishment for all crimes was death.

Solon, 594 B.C. He was one of the wisest lawgivers of any age or country. He abolished the offensive laws of Draco. His laws provided:

1. For the relief of the poorer people from the tyranny of the aristocracy.
2. For the abolition of oppressive rates of interest and of slavery for debt.
3. That the people should be divided into four classes according to their wealth, and that only those who owned property could be elected to office. This substituted a property qualification for mere accident of birth as a condition of State preferment.
4. That the entire people should have the right of suffrage whether they had property or not.
5. That a council of 400 be chosen annually to consider all questions to be submitted to the General Assembly.
6. That all questions of peace or war, the election of magistrates, and the decision of disputed law cases should be referred to the Ecclesia, or General Assembly of the people. Plutarch states that Solon made some of his laws intentionally obscure in order that the whole of the citizens might ultimately be called upon to vote on disputed questions as the final court of appeal.
7. He re-established the Areopagus as the high court of Athens, named after the hill on which it met. This court became the most famous in the world and was consulted largely by other nations.

THIRD TOPIC.

ATHENS FROM THE FIRST OLYMPIC GAMES TILL THE PERSIAN INVASION.

1. The Olympic games formed so important an element in the development of Grecian character and the progress of Greek civilization that other events are dated from the first Olympiad.

* The uses of these games were threefold—1st. The uniting all Greeks by one sentiment of national pride, and the memory of a common race; 2ndly. The inculcation of hardy discipline of physical education throughout the state, by teaching that the body had its honors as well as the intellect—a theory conducive to health in peace—and in those ages when men fought hand to hand, and individual strength and skill were the nerves of the army, to success in war; but 3rdly, and principally, its uses were in sustaining and feeding, as a passion, as a motive, as an irresistible incentive, the desire of glory. That desire spread through all classes; it animated all tribes; it taught that true rewards are not in gold and gems, but in men's opinions. The ambition of the Altis established fame as a common principle of action. What chivalry did for the few, the Olympic contests effected for the many—they made a knighthood of a people."—*Bulwer.*

2. Changes in Government.

1. The hereditary archons ruled from 1045 to 752 B.C. Then the elective element was introduced, and Athens became in a sense a republic with rulers still named archons, elected for ten years. They were chosen from the family of Codrus, and the aristocracy still ruled. There were seven decennial archons in all.

2. Annual archons were chosen from 683 B.C.

3. The people gradually began to resist the tyranny of the aristocracy, and the aristocratic factions themselves formed factions, so that a constitution became necessary to reconcile conflicting parties and unify the various elements of the state. Solon was chosen archon, and he laid the foundation of the true greatness of Athens. He introduced his constitution in 594 B.C.

4. REVOLUTION OF PEISISTRATUS. Taking advantage of the rivalry of opposing parties Peisistratus seized the government of Athens 560 B.C. and ruled with two interruptions till his death, 527 B.C. He was a very able man and a wise ruler. Solon used all his eloquence to prevent the submission of the people even to a considerate despot, but to no avail. Peisistratus was a patron of learning and art; he erected fine public buildings, and founded the first library in Athens. His sons Hippias and Hipparchus succeeded him. Hipparchus was murdered, and Hippias was expelled by the Alcmæonidæ

who had been driven out by Peisistratus, but who now returned, aided by the Spartans, and defeated Hippias who retired to Persia. He was afterward killed at the battle of Marathon.

5. TRIUMPH OF DEMOCRACY. After the expulsion of Hippias the aristocratic party led by Isagoras and supported by the Spartan king Cleomenes tried to secure control of the government. A leader of the people came from the noble family of Alcmæonidæ in the person of Cleisthenes. He succeeded in driving Cleomenes from Athens and completed the work begun by Solon in freeing the people. He divided the nation into ten districts each of which sent fifty men to the Council of Five Hundred, which became the parliament of Athens. This good work was accomplished 507 B.C.

Speaking of the democratic victory under Cleisthenes, Herodotus says:

"The Athenians then grew mighty, and it became plain that liberty is a brave thing."

"By the events which followed the expulsion of Hippias, the government of Athens had become at length substantially popular. All its former revolutions were but changes in the ruling portion of the nobility: sometimes, indeed, the weaker party called the people to its aid; but the people, though it might determine the struggle, gained little by it beyond the hope of better masters. No lasting security for good government was obtained, and any immediate improvement of administration depended on the personal character of the new rulers, and the degree in which they yet needed popular support against their beaten opponents. Such might again have been the result, if Cleisthenes had enjoyed his first victory undisputed; but by the strength of his enemies, and the determination of Cleomenes to set up an oligarchy, with Isagoras for its chief, his cause was permanently identified both with that of democracy and of Athenian independence. The middle and lower people, hitherto powerless through inexperience, inertness, and disunion, had numbers that might have made them superior both in votes of the assembly and in trials of force; they wanted leaders whose personal influence could keep them united, whose political experience might direct their conduct, and who might be obliged, instead of using the people as instruments to serve a temporary purpose in raising a faction, to rest their hopes on their continued activity."—*Mulkins.*

FOURTH TOPIC.

SPARTA FROM THE TIME OF LYCURGUS TO THE PERSIAN INVASION.

1. The history of Sparta during this period records no internal revolutions such as characterized Athens. The social democracy of Lycurgus was so broad that it required little extension. Sparta gradually increased her power until at the beginning of the fifth century before Christ she was the dominant power in the Peloponnesus and had no rival but Athens for the supremacy of Greece.

2. **Messenian Wars.**

The wars with Messenia were the chief wars of Sparta before 500 B.C. The first lasted from 743 to 723 B.C. and the second from 679 to 668 B.C. In both of these Sparta was successful. Messenian leaders: Aristodemus in first, and Aristomenes in second. The Messenians revolted a third time 464 B.C., but they were again subdued 454 B.C.

FIFTH TOPIC.

THE PERSIAN WAR.

1. **Causes of the War.**

There were many Grecian colonies on the west of Asia Minor. These had been conquered by the Persians. Some of them revolted and received aid from Athens. The Persians resented this interference with the extension of their empire, and Darius determined to add to his Asiatic dominions a portion of Europe. Hippias, the exiled ruler of Athens, helped to induce Darius to invade Greece.

2. First Invasion, 492 B.C.

Macedonia conquered, but the Persian fleet was wrecked off Mount Athos, and the army defeated by the Thracians. Persian leader Mardonius.

3. Second Invasion.

Datis and Artaphernes succeeded in landing a large army in Greece, and had got within twenty-two miles of Athens when they were met by Miltiades with an army of ten thousand Athenians and one thousand Plataeans at Marathon and utterly routed, 490 B.C.

This battle has been called "the birthday of Athenian greatness." It was a marvellous victory, and at once placed Athens on a par with Sparta as a military nation.

> "The Athenians reaped another important advantage from their victory; for on the field of Marathon the life, the hopes, and the hearts of the Pisistratidæ were utterly extinguished. At Marathon, the exiled Hippias, the last of his family, the instigator of the invasion, fell; and with him fell the fears of the Athenian people. Athens was now regarded among the states of Greece as equal, if not superior, in patriotism and valor even to Sparta herself." — *Ottley*.

4. Third Invasion.

Darius died before he was ready to avenge the defeat at Marathon, but ten years after that battle his son Xerxes invaded Greece with an army of 1,700,000 men and a fleet of more than 1200 ships. The Athenians were led by Themistocles and Aristides. Themistocles had planned to make the war chiefly a naval contest. The Spartans commanded the Greeks on land and Themistocles on the sea.

Xerxes was met in the pass of Thermopylæ, 480 B.C., by Leonidas, King of Sparta, leader of the Greeks, and held at bay until a traitor, Ephialtes, led the Persians by a path over the mountains, and threatened the Greeks in the rear. Leonidas promptly sent home all the Grecians except his 300 Spartans and 700 Thespians who would not leave him. The heroes who remained fought desperately until they met heroic death. Xerxes burned Athens, but his fleet was defeated at Salamis 480 B.C. Xerxes returned with part of his army by way of the Hellespont, and left Mardonius in Thessaly for the winter. Next year Mardonius invaded Greece. He destroyed the partially rebuilt city of Athens, and then retired to Bœotia, where his army was almost annihilated by Pausanius (Spartan) and Aristides (Athenian), 479 B.C. On the same day that Platæa was fought a great naval victory was won by the Greeks at Mycale under Leotychides (Spartan) and Xanthippus (Athenian). These victories were decisive. The Persians gave up the contest, and not only Greece but Macedon and Thrace were freed from Asiatic domination.

The effect of the Persian wars on Greece was beneficial. It gave the Greeks faith in themselves, and developed a spirit of unity among the different Greek states. "A small country had withstood the attack of half a continent: it had not only saved the most costly possessions that were endangered, its freedom, its independence; it felt itself strong enough to continue the contest, and did not lay aside its arms till it was permitted to prescribe the conditions of peace."

> "From a multitude of small states, never united, but continually distracted by civil broils—and such at the beginning of this period were the states of Greece—anything important could hardly be expected without the occurrence of some external event, which, by rallying the divided forces round one point, and directing them towards one object, should hinder them from mutually exhausting one another. It was the hostile attempts of Persia that first laid the foundation of the future splendour of Greece; certain states then grew so rapidly in power, that upon their particular history hinges the general history of all the rest."—*Heeren.*

Another consequence of the war was the great increase in the power of Athens. Her ascendancy among the states of Greece began with Marathon, and was firmly established by Themistocles and Aristides.

SIXTH TOPIC.

THE ATHENIAN ASCENDANCY.

1. From the close of the Persian wars till near the close of the Peloponnesian war Athens was supreme in Grecian affairs. Her greatest glory was reached during these seventy years.

2. Leaders: Themistocles, Aristides, Cimon (son of Miltiades), Pericles and Alcibiades.

3. Establishment of a common fleet and a general treasury for Greece, under control of Athens.

4. The war against Persia did not end with the double defeat at Platæa and Mycale. The Greeks became invaders instead of defenders, and the war continued with intervals until 449 B.C. In 466 B.C. Cimon won a great victory at Eurymedon, defeating the Persians both by land and sea. Again, in 450 B.C., he organized an expedition and the war was brought to a close by the defeat of the Persians at Salamis, 449 B.C.

> "The fear of losing the whole island compelled Artaxerxes I. to sign a treaty of peace with Athens, in which he recognized the independence of the Asiatic Greeks, and agreed that his fleet should not navigate the Ægean Sea, nor his troops approach within three days' march of the coast."—*Hermann.*

5. **Wars between Greek States.**

About the middle of the fifth century before Christ several minor wars occurred. Some of the smaller states rebelled against paying tribute to Athens, and they were made subjects instead of allies. A sacred war between the Phocians and the Delphians for the possession of the oracle at Delphi in which Sparta assisted the Delphians and Athens the Phocians, was won by the Phocians. Corinth and Megara dispute about their boundary. Athens aids Megara and Sparta Corinth. Athens first defeated, ultimately victorious. Sparta, to weaken Athens, helped the Dorians against the Phocians. Spartans won at Tanagra, 457 B.C., but Athens won Œnophyta, 456 B.C. In 447 B.C. the Bœotians defeat the Athenians at Coronea. Euboea and Megara revolt, but are subdued. In 445 B.C. a truce was made between Athens and Sparta. It was to last thirty years, but ended in fourteen years.

"The conclusion of peace with Persia, glorious as it was, and the death of the man whose grand political object was to preserve union among the Greeks, again roused the spirit of internal strife. For notwithstanding nearly twenty years intervened before the tempest burst with all its fury, this period was so turbulent during its course that Greece seldom enjoyed universal peace. While Athens, by her naval strength, was maintaining her ascendancy over the confederates, and while some of those confederates were raising the standard of rebellion, and passing over to Sparta, everything was gradually combining towards the formation of a counter-league, the necessary consequence of which must have been a war, such as the Peloponnesian."—*Carr*.

6. **The Age of Pericles.**

Most brilliant in the history of Athens, or Greece. More great men in proportion to the population than at any other period or in any other country. Under Cimon, Athens had been beautified by many elegant buildings and fine gardens, and its long walls had been built for four miles, connecting it with the sea. During the period of the rule of Pericles Athens reached the climax of her wealth and power. Her great naval ascendancy brought her the treasures of surrounding nations; literature, art and education flourished. Pericles himself one of the most striking characters of history.

SEVENTH TOPIC.

THE PELOPONNESIAN WAR, FROM 431 B.C. TO 404 B.C.

1. **Causes.**

Rivalry between Athens and Sparta; discontent of smaller states at the arrogance of the Athenians; fear that Athens would make other states subjects instead of allies; opposition between aristocracy and democracy. The immediate cause

of the great war was a quarrel between Corinth and her
colony Corcyra. Athens favored Corcyra. Sparta sided
with Corinth, and ultimately nearly all the Greek states and
colonies became engaged.

2. **Athenian allies.**

All the islands of the Ægean (except Melos and Thera), Corcyra,
Zacynthus, Chios, Lesbos, Samos; the Greek colonies on the
coast of Asia Minor, and on the shores of Thrace and
Macedon; Naupactus, Platæa, and some places of Acarnania.

3. **Spartan allies.**

All the Peloponnesus, except Argos and Achaia, which stood
neutral; Bœotia, Locris, Phocis, and Megara, Ambracia,
Anactorium, and the island of Leucas.

4. **Course of the War.**

First: Ten years of indecisive warfare ending with a truce of fifty
years, which, though not formally set aside till 415 B.C., was
violated almost as soon as it was arranged.

Second: The invasion of Sicily by Athens. Planned by Alcibiades. Greatest expedition sent out by Athens. Alcibiades
recalled. His desertion to Sparta. Athenian defeat at
Syracuse, 413 B.C., broke the power of Athens in a single
day. Grote calls this "the most picturesque event in
history." Athens had sent her greatest army and fleet
under one of her most brilliant sons, a nephew of the noble
Pericles, but had foolishly humiliated him and transformed
him into an enemy.

Third: Struggle of Athens to regain her lost ascendancy for
about ten years. Athens, still leader in literature and art,
made heroic but vain efforts to get back the proud position
she lost at Syracuse. Alcibiades was forgiven and recalled,
and for about five years success came to the Athenians.
The government at home was unsettled and again Alcibiades
was banished, 407 B.C. He was murdered in Asia in 404
B.C. Lysander annihilated the Athenian fleet, 405 B.C., at
Ægospotami.

"It was made known at Piræus by the consecrated ship *Paralus*, which arrived there during the night, coming straight from the Hellespont. Such a moment of distress and agony had never been experienced in Athens. The terrible disaster of Sicily had become known to the people by degrees without any authorized reporter ; but here was the official messenger, fresh from the scene, leaving no doubt or room to question the magnitude of the disaster, or the irretrievable ruin impending over the city. The wailings and cries of grief, first arising in Piræus, were transmitted by the guards stationed on the Long Walls up to the city."—*Grote*.

Next year, 404 B.C., Athens surrendered to Sparta after a siege of four months. The democracy was overthrown, and Sparta was the leader among the states of Greece.

Lysias, the Athenian orator, expressed the feelings of Athens when he said : "Greece, on the fall of Athens, should have shorn her hair, and mourned at the tomb of her heroes, as over the sepulture of Liberty herself."

EIGHTH TOPIC.

FROM THE CLOSE OF THE PELOPONNESIAN WAR TO THE CLOSE OF THE THEBAN WAR.

1. The Spartans under Lysander organized the Athenian government by the "Thirty Tyrants." Many Athenians exiled or put to death. Within a year Thrasybulus organized the Athenian exiles in Thebes and drove out the "Thirty" and re-established the constitution of Solon.

2. "The Retreat of the Ten Thousand." Cyrus rebelled against his brother Artaxerxes, the king of Persia, and engaged a large body of Greeks to aid him. Battle of Cunaxa, 401 B.C. Defeat and death of Cyrus. Retreat of the "Ten Thousand Greeks" under Xenophon.

3. The weakness of the Athenians is shown by the impeachment and death of Socrates, 339 B.C.

4. Attempt of Agesilaus, king of Sparta, to conquer Persia, 396-394 B.C. Successful till Persia stirred up a war at home and Agesilaus had to return.

5. The Corinthian War.

Corinth, Thebes, Athens and Argos united against Sparta.

"The tyranny of Sparta, and more particularly the recent devastation of Elis, was the alleged pretext; but the bribes of Timocrates, the Persian envoy, were the real causes of this war."—*Abbott.*

Agesilaus defeats the Corinthians and their allies at Coronea, 394 B.C., but the Athenian and Persian fleets under Conon destroyed the Spartan fleet at Cnidus, 394 B.C.

6.
Conon for a time made Athens mistress of the sea, and began to rebuild the walls of Athens.

7.
Antalcidas, a Spartan, arranged a humiliating peace with Persia, 387 B.C., by which the alliance between Persia and Athens was broken off, and Persia was allowed to retain most of the Greek colonies.

8. The Theban War.

In the Olynthian war the Spartans seized the Cadmea, or Acropolis, of Thebes, 382 B.C. It was re-captured by Pelopidas in 379 B.C., and the Thebans under Epaminondas and Pelopidas became leaders of those states that wished to be free from the grinding tyranny of Sparta. The Spartans defeated by Epaminondas at Leuctra, 371 B.C. Four invasions of the Peloponnesians by the Thebans followed. In the fourth the Spartans were again defeated in the battle of Mantinea, 362 B.C. Epaminondas was killed just as the victory was achieved. Peace followed in 361 B.C. The power of Sparta was broken and the power of Thebes established by one man. Theban sway did not last long after the death of Epaminondas. He raised Thebes to the position of honor, but it fell with him.

"Cicero pronounces him to be the first man of Greece. The judgment of Polybius, though not summed up so emphatically in a single epithet is delivered in a manner hardly less significant and laudatory: 'The best men of action, combining the soldier and patriot—such as Timoleon and Philopoemen—set before them Epaminondas as their model. With him the dignity of Thebes both began and ended.'"—*Grote.*

NINTH TOPIC.

PHILIP OF MACEDON.

1. The people of Greece were exhausted by long continued fighting among themselves, yet instead of conserving their powers they entered, in 356 B.C., on a war of ten years, called the Phocian, or First Sacred war.
2. Philip of Macedon came to the throne 359 B.C. He saw clearly the weakened condition of Greece, and interfered in the Phocian war against the Phocians, whose country he devastated. He was admitted to the Amphictyonic Council with the two votes formerly held by the Phocians.
3. Demosthenes arouses Athens against Philip. Æschines defends Philip.
4. Philip became general of the Amphictyonic Council, and marched into Greece to make war on the Locrians for alleged sacrilege. The Athenians and Thebans regarded this Second Sacred war as a pretext for overthrowing the liberties of Greece. They raised an army and met Philip at Chæronea, 338 B.C., where they were defeated and the independence of Greece was extinguished.

TENTH TOPIC.

GREAT NAMES OF GREEK LITERATURE.

1. During the legendary period: Homer and Hesiod.
2. **Lyric Poets.**
    Alcaeus and Sappho. In prime about 600 B.C.
    > "Sappho's poetry stands highest in the passionate lyrics of all times and ages."—*Jevons*.

    Anacreon, 560 B.C.
    Simonides, 556 B.C.
    Pindar, 521 B.C.

3. **Dramatists.**
   a. **Tragedy:**
      Æschylus, 525 B.C.
      Sophocles, 495 B.C.
      Euripides, 485 B.C.

   b. **Comedy:**
      Aristophanes, 444 B.C.
      Alexis, 390 B.C.

4. **Historians.**
   Herodotus, about 485 B.C.
   Thucydides, about 472 B.C.
   Xenophen, 429 B.C.

5. **Orators.**
   Lysias, 458 B.C.
   Antisthenes, about 450 B.C.
   Isocrates, 436 B C.
   Demosthenes, 383 B.C.
   Hyperides, } Contemporaries of Demosthenes
   Æschines

6. **Philosophers.**
   Thales, about 636 B.C.
   Pythagoras, 540 B.C.
   Socrates, 469 B.C.
   Plato, 429 B.C.

A TOPICAL ANALYSIS

OF

ROMAN HISTORY.

FIRST TOPIC.

THE MONARCHY, 753 B.C. TO 509 B.C.

1. "Exaggerated and embellished as the most ancient traditions of the Romans respecting their origin may be, they all agree in this—that the Romans belonged to the race of the Latins, and that their city was a colony of the neighboring Alba Longa."—*Heeren.*

   Niebuhr says that thirty Latin towns were controlled by Alba, and that Rome, Quirium and Lucerum became one. Lucerum was an Etruscan town and its people did not gain equal standing with the citizens of the other two towns until the time of Tarquin I. These three tribes are known as the Ramnes, Tities and Luceres.

2. Seven kings are said to have ruled in Rome:
   Romulus, 753 B.C.
   Numa Pompilius, 715 B.C.
   Tullus Hostilius, 673 B.C.
   Ancus Martius, 642 B.C.
   Tarquinius Priscus, 616 B.C.
   Servius Tullius, 578 B.C.
   Tarquinius Superbus, 534–509 B.C.

3. **Romulus.**
   Roman wall built. Union of Romans and Sabines. Two kings till the death of Tatius, the Sabine king.

4. **Numa Pompilius.**

   Romans and Sabines could not agree on death of Romulus. No king for a year, senators ruling in turn, ten at a time for five days. Numa Pompilius, a Sabine, elected by the Romans. Founding of religious institutions in Rome.

5. **Tullus Hostilius.**

   A Roman elected by the Sabines. Destruction of Alba, the head of the thirty Latin cities, and transfer of her power to Rome. Settlement of leading Alban families in Rome.

6. **Ancus Martius.**

   A Sabine elected by the Romans. Latin wars. Extension of Roman territory. Encouragement of agriculture.

7. **Tarquinius Priscus.**

   Great public works, public buildings, drains, etc. Senate increased from 200 to 300, probably by allowing the Etruscan Luceres the same rights as the Ramnes and Tities.

8. **Servius Tullius.**

   Great extension of the empire. Servian constitution. Plebs recognized in Comitia Tributa, and Comitia Centuriata, a new assembly instituted, based on the new organization of the army on the basis of land ownership instead of birth. Erection of the Servian wall around the Palatine and the Quirinal cities, and adjoining settlements. Beginning of Latin colonization.

9. **Tarquinius Superbus.**

   Overthrow of the Servian constitution. Tyranny of Tarquin. Treachery of Sextus. Expulsion of the Tarquins and end of monarchy.

   > "The evils of the tyranny of Tarquin survived him; it was not so easy to restore what he had destroyed as to expel him and his family; the commons no longer stood beside the patricians as an equal order—free, wealthy, well armed, and well organized; they were now poor, ill armed, and with no bonds of union; they therefore naturally sank beneath the power of the nobility, and the revolution which drove out the Tarquins established at Rome, not a free commonwealth, but an exclusive and tyrannical aristocracy."—*Arnold*.

10. Government.

The government during the monarchy was vested in (a) The king, who commanded in war and administered justice; (b) The senate nominated by the king; (c) The Populus, or Patrician citizens; (d) The Plebs, first recognized by Servius Tullus.

The Populus held its meetings (comitia curiata) in the Comitium, an open space in the city.

11. Patricians and Plebeians.

The citizens of Rome were divided into two distinct classes: the patricians and the plebeians.

The patricians were the aristocratic families of Rome, originally freeborn citizens who were independent landowners. The patricians at first formed the state. The term populus applied to the patricians, patres or fathers only.

The plebeians were the common people who gradually came to settle in Rome, and who were "subjects of the Roman state, but not members of it." They greatly increased by additions from conquered Latin cities. Many of the wealthy citizens of other Latin states came to Rome as it increased in power, so that the plebs were not necessarily poorer than the patricians. They had no share in the government of the city till the time of Servius Tullius, and the second Tarquin took away from them the power given by the Servian law.

SECOND TOPIC.

FROM THE OVERTHROW OF THE MONARCHY TO THE PUNIC WARS, 509 B.C. TO 264 B.C.

1. Titles of Leading Officials.

Consuls, first named practors, two elected annually instead of a king; first appointed, 509 B.C.

Dictators, men chosen in times of special danger and ch... with supreme authority, first appointed, 501 B.C.

Tribunes, guardians of the rights of the plebs; first appointed 494 B.C.

Quaestors, or finance officers; first appointed, 509 B.C.

Censors, appointed to perform some of the duties of consuls, 443 B.C. (Budget, muster-roll, and filling vacancies in senate and equites).

2. Leaders during the Period.

Spurius Cassius, consul.

    (a) Renewed league with Latins, 493 B.C.
    (b) Made league with Hernicans, 486 B.C.
-   (c) First Agrarian Law, 486 B.C.

Cincinnatus—great dictator in Æquian wars.

- Genucius—leader of plebs in securing enforcement of Agrarian Laws. Murdered 473 B.C.

Publilius Volero—"second great charter," 471 B.C.

- Terentilius—led to revision of laws, 462 B.C.

- Icilius—law to prevent interruption to tribunes when addressing the plebs, 492 B.C. Distribution of land to poor citizens for building lots, 466 B.C.

- Valerius and Horatius—liberal lawgivers, 449 B.C.

Camillus—five times dictator.

- Canulius—laws sanctioning marriage between patricians and plebs, and substituting military tribunes for consuls.

- Licinius (with whom was associated Sextius—Rome's greatest reformer, passed Licinian laws, after a long struggle, in 367 B.C.

- Sextius—first plebeian consul, 366 B.C.

Marcius Rutilus—first plebeian chosen dictator, 356 B.C., and first plebeian censor, 351 B.C.

- Publilius Philo, B.C. 339 dictator and lawgiver.

3. Constitutional Growth.

Mainly a struggle for equality between plebeians and patricians. Plebs coerce the patricians by refusing to fight. Ultimate success of the plebs. Tribunes elected to protect the plebs, 594 B.C. At first two, afterwards five, finally ten. Plebiscita passed by assembled plebs, to have force among the plebs themselves.

> "The character of the Tribunes, was, in every respect, different from that of the consuls. The appearance of the former was modest and humble; but their persons were sacred and inviolable. Their force was suited rather for opposition than for action. They were instituted to defend the oppressed, to pardon offences, to arraign the enemies of the people, and, when they judged it necessary, to stop, by a single word, the whole machine of government. As long as the republic subsisted, the dangerous influence, which either the consul or the tribune might derive from their respective jurisdiction, was diminished by several important restrictions. Their authority expired with the year in which they were elected; the former office was divided between ten, the latter among two persons; and as both in their private and public interest they were averse to each other, their mutual conflicts contributed for the most part to strengthen, rather than destroy, the balance of the constitution."—*Grote.*

Agrarian laws. The extension of the territory as well as the social and economical condition of the people rendered the enactment of land laws necessary. The agrarian laws were closely associated with the growth of freedom. The first was enacted by Spurius Cassius in 486 B.C. It was a long time before it was properly executed by the consuls owing to the patrician opposition. It provided that part of the public lands be leased for the public treasury and part given to the needy.

The Publilian law increased power of plebs, and provided for election of tribunes by the plebeians by tribes, and not by the whole people in centuries, as this gave the patricians too much control through their clients.

The Terentilian law proposed to limit the consular power and to appoint ten commissioners to prepare laws for all classes. The law was violently opposed, but at length the decemvirs were appointed, 451 B.C. They codified the laws in twelve tables. The decemvirs ruled in place of consuls and tribunes, and their tyranny became so offensive (story of Appius Claudius and Virginia) that the plebs retired a second time to Mons Sacer, and the consuls and tribunes were re-appointed.

"With regard to the constitution, there cannot be any doubt that the *laws of the Twelve Tables* contained an arrangement by which the whole body of Roman citizens, the patricians and their clients, as well as the plebeians, henceforth became members of the thirty local Plebeian tribes. *The Comitia Tributa*, therefore, instead of a merely plebeian, became a national assembly for legislative purposes, but the measures passed by it still required the sanction of the curia; it had also the election of all minor magistrates, as the aediles, quaestors and tribunes, and was at the same time the high court of appeal."—*Schmitz*

The Valerio-Horatian laws, 449 B.C., greatly increased the legal force of the plebiscita, or resolutions of the plebs. The plebs became equal with the centuries in right of legal enactment

The Canulian laws gave social recognition to the plebs by authorizing marriages between plebs and patricians, and opened the consulship to plebs by recognizing military tribunes. From 445 to 367 B.C., there were sometimes consuls and sometimes military tribunes.

In 443 B.C. the power of the consuls, or military tribunes, was limited by the appointment of *Censors*, who—
  (*a*) Managed the budget and muster-rolls.
  (*b*) Filled vacancies in the Senate and Equites.

In 421 B.C. questors are increased from two to four, and plebs granted the right to be questors. In 409 B.C. three of the four were plebeian.

In 385 B.C. the Latin league was closed against new members. The Latin confederacy now includes: thirty cities with full rights, and seventeen without the right of voting.

In 367 B.C. the Licinian laws were passed, after a struggle of ten years led by Licinius and Sextius. Rome's true reform bill.

Provisions:
  (*a*) Relief of debtors (great distress had prevailed).

(b) Restriction of land to be held by one citizen to 500 jugera of public land, and removal of the right to feed on common pasture more than 100 oxen and 500 sheep.

(c) Compulsory employment of a certain proportion of free laborers.

(d) Restoration of consulship with the provision that *one consul must be a pleb*. (This law was sometimes violated).

(e) Curtailment of power of consuls by appointment of a *praetor* to administer justice, and curule Ædiles to act as policemen.

The result of these laws was to break down in a large measure the opposition between the patricians and the plebs.

In 357 B.C. interest reduced to ten per cent., and the rich first taxed.

In 317 B.C. interest reduced to 5 per cent., and in 342 it was abolished.

In 339 Publilius passed three laws:

(a) Confirming and enlarging the legislative power of the plebs.

(b) Defining and limiting the power of the senate over the comitia centuriata.

(c) Providing that *one Censor must be a plebeian*.

In 326 imprisonment for debt was limited.

In 287 B.C. the Hortensian law finally established the legislative authority of the plebs in tribal assembly, and abolished the veto power of the senate.

> "Henceforth the decree of the plebs on the rogatis of a tribune has the same force as the decree of the populus on the rogatis of a consul."

> "AFTER THE PASSING OF THE HORTENSIAN LAW, THE POLITICAL DISTINCTION BETWEEN PATRICIANS AND PLEBEIANS CEASED, *and, with a few unimportant exceptions, both orders were placed on a footing of perfect equality.* Henceforth the name Populus is sometimes applied to the plebeians alone, and sometimes to the whole body of Roman citizens, as assembled in the comitia centuriata, or tributa."—*Arnold.*

"The gradual and most perfect separation which can be traced in any age or country between the nation and the people, as marked that of the patricians and the plebeians, as it was not established to the time of the Roman republic. Wealth and honors, the offices of the state and the ceremonies of religion, were almost exclusively possessed by the former, who, preserving the purity of their blood with the most insulting jealousy, held their clients in a condition of oppressive vassalage; but these distinctions, so incompatible with the spirit of a free people, were removed, after a long struggle, by the persevering efforts of the tribunes."—*Grote.*

4. Leading Wars.

The power of Rome gradually extended with these until it controlled all Italy. It took nearly two and a half centuries to accomplish this result.

The Etruscans take Rome, 508 B.C.

Latin war, Battle of Lake Regillus, 498 B.C. (493 B.C. also given). First dictator.

Wars with Æquians and Volscians lasting with intervals for about fifty years, 489–431 B.C. Cincinnatus, Appius Claudius, Camillus. Power of Æquians and Volscians broken at length, 431 B.C., by Romans, Latins and Hernicans.

Conquest of Veii, 396 B.C.

Rome taken by Gauls, except the Capitol saved by Manlius, 390 B.C. The Gauls leave Rome for a ransom.

Volscians take advantage of Rome's defeat by Gaul, and make war, 389 B.C., aided now by Latins and Hernicans, but Camillus defeats them.

Etruscans defeated by C. Marcus Rutilus, first plebeian dictator 356–351 B.C.

The Samnite wars began 343 B.C. and lasted more than fifty years, with brief interruptions. The Romans were aided by the Latins and Campanians. Three distinct wars were fought. First began 343 B.C.; second 327 B.C., and third 298 B.C. Romans defeated in second in early part of war, but Samnites and allies beaten and forced to sue suit, 304 B.C. Last Samnian war fought for eight years with desperation, but the Samnians and their allies were everywhere defeated. Chief battles Clusium and Sentinum.

Niebuhr calls the march of the Samnites into Etruria "one of the most brilliant feats in ancient history."

> "The war lasted eight years, and was even more destructive to the Samnites than the earlier ones; but they conducted it with great vigour, and their whole plan, though not crowned with success, is one of the grandest recorded in history."—*Niebuhr.*

The war with Tarentum was the last great struggle of Rome for the complete control of Italy. From 281 to 271 the war continued. Pyrrhus, king of Epirus, aided the Tarentines.

In 266 B.C. Rome was master of all Italy. The last peoples to submit were the Sarsinates and Sallentini.

5. Relation of Rome to the Italian nations.

> "Rome thus became the most powerful and compact state that then existed. The nations retained their own administrations, laws, languages, and dialects, but Rome was their central point, and they were gradually to rub off what was foreign to, and irreconcilable with, that centre."—*Niebuhr.*

Rome had sole right to make war, conclude treaties, and coin money. All Italian nations had to furnish contingents in war.

The other nations held varied relationships to Rome:

(*a*) Some had full citizenship, as:
  Those placed on public land.
  Incorporated communities, as Tusculum and the Sabine towns.
  Maritime colonies.

(*b*) Latin towns retaining autonomy and equality, but restricted in franchise and rights of migration.

(*c*) Citizens subject to taxation and service in the legions instead of with the allies.

(*d*) Other communities allied on varied terms, but all bound to supply contingents in war.

THIRD TOPIC.

THE PUNIC WARS.

1. Carthage and Rome came into conflict in Sicily. Carthage had been extending her power gradually, and almost to seize Sicily. Rome, having finished the conquest of Italy, was ready to check Carthage. Mamertines ask assistance of Rome at Messana. Rome consents. Carthage and Sicily oppose Rome.

2. **First Punic War, 264 to 241 B.C.**
   Romans under Appius Claudius successful in Sicily against Carthaginians and Hiero, king of Syracuse. Hiero enters into alliance with Rome, 263 B.C. Carthage controls sea. Romans raise a fleet and win first naval victory (by boarding bridges) 260 B.C. Carthage beaten in Corsica and Sardinia, 259 B.C. Romans under Regulus invade Africa, 256 B.C. Carthaginian fleet defeated at Ecnomus. Siege of Carthage. Regulus defeated by Xanthippus, and his army almost totally destroyed, 255 B.C. Roman fleet of 350 vessels nearly all lost by storm when returning with remnant of the army of Regulus. New fleet built and Northern Sicily conquered, 254 B.C., but the fleet nearly all lost in an invasion of Africa, 253 B.C. Roman victory by Metellus at Panormus, 250 B.C. Carthage won her only naval victory at Drepanum, 249 B.C. Hamilcar appointed Carthaginian general, 247 B.C., was successful in Sicily and on the coast of Southern Italy, but the defeat of Hanno at the Aegates Islands in 242 B.C. by the Roman fleet under Catulus leads to peace in 241 B.C. The Carthaginians leave Sicily, and pay a large sum to Rome, and Sicily, with the exception of the part ruled by Hiero, becomes the FIRST ROMAN PROVINCE.

3. **Second Punic War, 218 to 202 B.C.**
   The Carthaginians had devoted themselves for thirty years to strengthening their empire in Spain. In 218 B.C. Hannibal took Saguntum. Rome declared war. Hannibal marched to

Italy, crossing the Alps. Great Carthaginian victories at Ticinus and Trebia, 218 B.C. Terrible slaughter of Roman army at Trasimene. 217 B.C. Defeat of both consuls. Paulus and Varro, at Cannæ, 216 B.C. Capua and Southern Italy join Hannibal. Niebuhr says: "The number of the dead at Cannæ, according to the lowest estimation, was 40,000 foot and 2,700 horse."

4. Failure of Hannibal to march on Rome.

In 215 B.C. Hannibal defeated by Marcellus, and the Romans victorious also in Spain and Sardinia. Hannibal forms an alliance with Philip of Macedon. In 214 and 213 B.C. no very important changes. In 212 B.C. Hannibal seized Tarentum. Romans besiege Capua, but their army destroyed. Hannibal retires, and Capua again besieged. In Syracuse the Romans are successful, but in Spain Hasdrubal defeats Scipio and drives Romans out south of Ebro. In 211 B.C. Capua surrendered. Cornelius Scipio (Africanus) appointed to command in Spain. In five years he had driven the Carthaginians out of Spain. In 207 B.C. Hasdrubal led an army from Spain to help Hannibal, but he was defeated and slain at Metaurus. In 205 B.C. Scipio decides to invade Carthage. He defeated the Carthaginians in 203 B.C., and Hannibal was forced to return from Italy. In 202 B.C. the final battle of the war was fought at Zama, and the power of Sparta was broken.

5. Third Punic War, 149 to 146 B.C.

Rome, led by Cato, decided that "Carthage must be destroyed." Massinissa's encroachments encouraged by Rome. Carthage protests, and war is declared. Another Scipio defeats Carthaginians, and Carthage is utterly destroyed.

> "By the treaty which terminated the second Punic war, Rome had bound Carthage, and had attached to her a vampire to suck her blood until she sank exhausted; I speak of the restless and ferocious Massinissa, who lived a century, to the utter despair of the Carthaginians."
>
> "The whole transaction with Carthage was a cursed and diabolical undertaking."—*Niebuhr.*

FOURTH TOPIC.

GENERAL PROGRESS OF ROME DURING THE PERIOD OF THE PUNIC WARS, 264 TO 146 B.C.

1. Wonderful recuperative power of Rome. Fleet after fleet, army after army were destroyed by the Carthaginians, but still new armies were ready to follow.

2. **Extension of the empire.**

    The Romans extended the empire eastward as well as westward during this first century after becoming masters of Italy. They conducted three wars against Macedon during this period, and Greece became subject to Rome in the same year that Carthage was levelled, 146 B.C. By the defeat of Antiochus, king of Syria, the foundation of Asiatic supremacy was also laid.

3. **Constitutional changes.**

    (a) The Comitia loses its influence. The Roman citizens become more numerous and more scattered, so that they do not meet in assembly as formerly.

    (b) The supreme influence of the senate. The senate becomes the only deliberative body. It becomes more and more representative of great families, both patrician and plebeian. The tribunes aid in extending the power of the senate. They have veto power and use it to restrict the action of magistrates when the senate opposes it. They lead the plebs in adopting measures recommended by the senate.

    The senate dealt with questions of foreign policy and finance. As these questions increase in importance the influence of the senate necessarily becomes greater.

    (c) The organization of provincial governments.

    (d) Last dictator (old style), 202 B.C.

    (e) Both consuls plebeian for the first time, 172 B.C.

4. Social changes.

(a) The farmers decreased by the demand for men to fight in the almost continuous wars, and by the importation of foreign corn.

(b) Great increase in wealth, especially after eastern wars; greater power of capitalists.

(c) Influence of commerce in deciding public policy.

(d) The influence of Greek culture began to be felt.

5. Wars of the period in addition to the Punic wars.

(a) Macedonian wars.

First, 214 to 205 B.C. Philip of Macedon enters into alliance with Hannibal, but does not give him very energetic support. Rome forms alliance with the Ætolians. In 211 Athens, Sparta, and Pergamus join the Roman-Ætolian league. In 205 Ætolia makes peace with Philip, and Rome follows the example of her ally.

Second Macedonian war, 200 to 196 B.C. Reasons: Extension of Philip's power dangerous to Rome.

Danger to Egypt affecting Roman trade. Rome's friendly relations with Greek cities.

Egypt, Rhodes, Pergamus, and commercial cities of Greece in alliance with Rome. Syrians, Acarnanians, and Bœotians on Philip's side.

In 198 B.C. the Achaeans and Epirus join Rome.

In 197 B.C. Flaminius defeats Philip at Cynoscephalæ, and in 196 peace is concluded. Philip surrenders all possessions in Asia Minor, Thrace, Greece, and the Ægean Islands, and pays 1000 talents to Rome. He also loses power to make foreign alliances without permission from Rome.

Third Macedonian war, 149 to 146 B.C.

Andriscus (Pseudo-Philip) defeats the Romans 149 B.C. but is defeated and captured 148 B.C. Macedonia becomes a Roman province, 148 B.C. In 147 B.C. the Achaean League invade Sparta, and decline to recognize Rome's authority to interfere, and in 146 B.C. Grecian liberty was overthrown by Mummius at Leucoptera, and by the destruction of Corinth. Rome their deadly rivals Carthage and Greece, in the same year.

(b) **War with Antiochus of Syria, 192 to 189 B.C.**

Antiochus the Great determined to conquer Europe, as Alexander the Great had at one time conquered Asia. Invaded Greece. Rome aided Greece, and drove him out of Europe. He was followed into Asia by Scipio Africanus and his brother, and defeated at Magnesia, 190 B.C. Peace was concluded 188 B.C. Antiochus gave to Rome 15,000 talents, relinquished all his claims to European possession, surrendered all his Asiatic territory west of the Halys and Mount Taurus, and was restricted in his rights of war and navigation. Rome formed most of the territory surrendered by Antiochus into the state of Pergamus, to form a check to Syria.

(c) **Wars with the Southern Gauls,** as allies of Carthage or independently, all ending in favor of Rome. Cisalpine Gaul subdued, 222 B.C. First Roman victory in Transalpine Gaul, 154 B.C.

(d) **Illyrian wars,** 230, 229 and 219 B.C., all favorable to Rome.

(e) **Ligurian wars,** lasting with intervals for more than twenty years, 185 to 163 B.C. Romans successful.

FIFTH TOPIC.

FROM THE END OF THE PUNIC WARS TO THE FIRST TRIUMVIRATE, 146 TO 60 B.C.

1. **Wars, and extension of territory.**

   (a) **Spanish war, 143 to 133 B.C.,** ending with the conquest of Spain. Numantia destroyed by Scipio Africanus (Numantinus) and inhabitants sold into slavery, 133 B.C.

   (b) **Revolt of slaves in Sicily, 135 to 132 B.C.**
   Seventy thousand slaves under Eunus and Cleon rose in rebellion, and for nearly four years defied Rome. They were finally conquered by Rupilius, 132 B.C.

(c) **Numidian war, 111 to 106 B.C.**

Jugurtha, king of Numidia, refused to recognize Roman authority in Africa. The Tribune Memmius roused the merchants of Rome, and against the majority of the senate secured the declaration of war against Jugurtha. Metellus and Marius lead the Roman army. Jugurtha made prisoner, and Numidia divided, 106 B.C.

(d) **The Cimbrian war, 113 to 101 B.C.**

The Cimbri and Teutones with 300,000 warriors came from the neighborhood of the Baltic Sea. They were the first of the great northern tribes to invade Roman territory. For nine years they were victorious. They devastated Gaul and Helvetia. In 105, at Aransio on the Rhone, 80,000 Romans were killed in one battle. In 102 B.C. Marius annihilated the Teutones at Aquæ Sextiæ; and in 101 he destroyed the Cimbrians near Verona, in the Raudine Plain.

"The Teutones were literally annhilated, for those who survived put an end to their own life."—*Niebuhr*.

(e) **The Social war, 90 to 88 B.C.**

This was a desperate struggle of the Italian states for Roman citizenship. Three hundred thousand Italians lost their lives. The Latin colonies remained true to Rome, and saved it from defeat. Sulla first won great fame in this war.

(f) **Civil war between Marius and Sulla, 88 to 82 B.C.**

Rome was deluged with blood by the rivalry of these two great generals. For the first time Rome was invaded by a Roman army. Sulla had been appointed to command the army against Mithridates. Marius, after Sulla's departure from the city, got himself appointed to the command. Sulla returned, and by the legions of Rome drove out the Marian party. He then proceeded to the East.

In 87 B.C. the Consul Cinna determined on the recall of Marius, but he was defeated by Octavius and driven from Rome. Cinna and Marius raised an army, and, after an extraordinary experience as a fugitive, Marius returned in triumph to Rome. There began a chronic butchery of his opponents.

"The victory which the rebels had thus gained was followed by the wildest cruelties. Marius had a body-guard of slaves whom he used to murder those whom he wished to get rid of. In this manner the most distinguished persons were despatched, especially his personal enemies. Among these unhappy victims was the celebrated orator, M Antonius. Q. Catulus, who had once been the colleague of Marius, put an end to his own life. No proscription took place, but the butchery was carried on to such an extent that at length even Cinna himself could bear it no longer; and he was instructed, by the advice of Sertorius, to put to death the band of servile assassins kept by Marius. On the sixteenth day after Marius had entered on his seventh consulship, he died, in the middle of January. The shedding of blood now ceased, but not the bitter spirit of the parties." Smith.

In January, 86 B.C., Marius died. Cinna remained leader in Rome, however, and maintained public opinion against Sulla. When Sulla had completed the first Mithridatic war he returned and defeated his Roman enemies the second time. In 82 B.C. the Roman people fully submitted to their army. Sulla was appointed dictator, and thousands of his opponents among the Roman leaders were put to death.

(g) **Mithraditic wars, 88 to 63 B.C.**

Mithridates, king of Pontus, ordered a massacre of the Romans in Asia Minor, and determined to free Asia from Roman power. While Roman factions were quarreling at home he seized Bithynia and Cappadocia, and took possession of Greece. Sulla took Athens, defeated Mithridates at Cheronea, 86 B.C., and at Orchomenus, 85 B.C., and concluded a peace with Mithridates, 84 B.C. Mithridates surrendered Bithynia and Cappadocia, gave eighty ships to Rome, and an indemnity of 3,000 talents. Mithridates renewed the war in 74 B.C., and was fairly successful for about ten years against Lucullus. Pompey was given supreme command in Asia in 66, and he speedily broke the power of the great king of Pontus, and established Roman authority in Asia. Mithridates died 63 B.C.

- **(h) Revolt of Spartacus, 73 to 71 B.C.**
    Spartacus, with a band of gladiators, escaped from Rome and raised an army of slaves and discontented Italians. For three years he threatened Rome, and defeated the armies sent against him. In 71 B.C. he was defeated by Crassus, and the remnant of his army was destroyed by Pompey, on his return from Spain.

2. **Constitutional Changes from 145 to 60 B.C.**
    - **(a) Loss of power by the Senate.**
        Two reasons lead to this result: Great popular agitators appeal directly to the people, and the generals of the army use their power to coerce the senate and people. The first example of this was the seizure of power by Sulla, in 88 B.C.
        In addition to these external causes there was an internal reason for the decay of the influence of the senate. The extension of Provincial Government led to senatorial corruption.
    - **(b) Rise of the Equites,** the party of wealth, who subordinated all other political ideals to commercial considerations. They were state contractors, bankers, money lenders and merchants. They were tax collectors also, and often bought the right to collect taxes, especially the taxes of Asia. The laws of Caius Gracchus, 123 B.C., gave the Equites a start towards power.
    - (c) Marius introduced two changes in regard to the army in 107 B.C.:
        - (1) Military appointments were made by the people instead of the senate.
        - (2) The army was made free to all citizens without regard to property.
    - **(d) Agrarian Laws.**
        In 133 B.C., Tiberius Gracchus saw the rapid decline of the farmer class, and introduced laws to prevent the occupation of too much land by the rich, and its equitable rental in small portions to the poor. Opposed by Octavius, his colleague, and the senate, he appealed to the people, and won his cause, but was killed in a riot, 133 B.C.

Ten years later, 123 B.C., Caius Gracchus proposed to renew the law of his brother, Tiberius, to give cheap corn to citizens for planting, and to found southern colonies, both in Italy and abroad. Little good resulted. The senate declared war on the Gracchan agitators and defeated them. Caius Gracchus induced one of his own slaves to put him to death.

In 119 B.C., a law was passed stopping further allotments and imposing a fixed rent.

In 111 B.C., all public land was converted into private property.

In 100 B.C., Marius, with the power of the army, forced the senate to consent to a new distribution of lands in Gaul, to establish new colonies, and to grant cheaper corn.

(e) Struggles for the franchise.

The Italian states wished for a share in the government of the country. They had to contribute money and soldiers for the empire, and they demanded citizenship. The proud Romans refused to grant their demands, and the Social War resulted. Though defeated by the Roman armies, the franchise was gradually extended to the Italians.

3. The Social Struggle.

The last hundred years of the Roman republic was marked by fierce class struggles. The aristocracy of family and the aristocracy of wealth united in resisting the efforts of the people for greater freedom. The old strife between the patricians and the plebs was continued in a new form. Unable to resist the measures of such liberal statesmen as the Gracchi by constitutional means, the senate resorted to the base use of force. The murder of Tiberius Gracchus and three hundred of his followers was the first civil bloodshed in Rome. This stupid attempt to destroy principles by murdering their advocates soon reacted on the senate itself. They put force above law, and in less than half a century Sulla used the Roman army as a force to dominate the Roman senate. The use of the army to control the constitutional law-making authority overthrew the republic. The Roman armies became agencies for the gratification of the personal ambitions of successful generals, until one of them became strong enough to concentrate in himself the complete control, and the republic was overthrown.

> "The luxury of the East, though united with Grecian taste, which had been introduced among the great by Lucellus; the immense riches poured into the treasury by Pompey; the tempting examples of unlimited power, which single citizens had already exercised; the purchase of the magistracy by individuals in order, like Verres, after the squandering of millions, to enrich themselves again in the provinces; the demands of soldiers upon their generals; and the ease with which an army might be raised by him who had only money enough to pay it; all these circumstances must have foreboded new and approaching convulsions; even if the preceding storms in this colossal republic, in which we must now judge of virtues and vices, as well as of riches and power, by a very magnified standard, had not formed men of that gigantic character they did."—*Heeren.*

4. Cataline's conspiracy, 65 to 62 B.C.

One of the most extensive attempts to make the whole machinery of Rome subordinate to the ambition of one man, was the conspiracy of Cataline. Cicero's orations led to his expulsion and ultimate defeat and death.

> "If Cataline really had any object at all, unless we suppose the crimes themselves to have been his object, it must have been that of making himself tyrant, and of becoming a second Sylla, without the intention, however, of ever resigning his tyranny."—*Niebuhr.*

5. The first triumvirate; Cæsar, Pompey and Crassus, 60 B.C.

Julius Cæsar, who had rapidly risen to power and had secured military renown and wealth in Spain.

Pompey, who had done more than any other man to extend the Roman empire, and had been given the most splendid triumph yet accorded in Rome, 62 B.C., for the conquest of twenty-one kings.

Crassus, the richest Roman.

Pompey and Cæsar had each been treated discourteously by the senate, and they decided to unite in order to secure the election of Cæsar as consul. The wealth of Crassus was necessary to bribe the people. Cæsar was elected Consul in spite of the opposition of the senate.

SIXTH PERIOD.

FROM 60 B.C. TO THE CLOSE OF THE REIGN OF AUGUSTUS.

1. Great men of the period.

Cato: A great leader of the patricians who stood bravely for republicanism in the midst of the conflicts of Cæsar and Pompey. He killed himself after the defeat of Scipio and the final triumph of Cæsar at Thapsus, 46 B.C.

> "If there be, indeed, a great man in Roman history who deserves his fame, it is Cato. He did not pay any regard to existing circumstances, and so made them worse. But his character was above blame. After Cato's death, Cicero wrote his celebrated 'Laudatio M. Catonis' would to heaven we had it still! He was the great hero of the Stoic philosophy."—*Niebuhr*.

Cicero: Rome's greatest orator. He exposed the conspiracy of Cataline, and was, after Cato, the last great leader of the republican party in the senate. His Philippics were uttered against Antony. When the second triumvirate was established on a safe basis by the proscription of the enemies of each of the triumvirs, Cicero was the first on the list of Antony. He was murdered, 43 B.C.

> "Cicero was a man of honour, far above the thought of anything like meanness. The consciousness of being able to give pleasure by talent was his highest delight. He was not a weak character, but he was a most impressible being, and of a morbid sensibility, and keenly alive to anything like a slight. The real spring-time of his life was the time of his prætorship and consulate."—*Niebuhr*

Pompey was a most successful commander. He did more than any other general to extend the Roman empire. Through the influence of Cato, who urged that it was better 'To choose a master than to wait for a tyrant whom enemies will impose upon us," Pompey was made the head of the patrician party, and sole consul, in order to check Cæsar, who was regarded as the leader of the elements opposed to the patrician senate. He was defeated by Cæsar at Pharsalia, 48 B.C., and afterwards murdered in Egypt.

"It is hard to speak of Pompey, as the outlines of his character are not marked. In his youth he was abler, but afterwards he was nothing great either as a statesman or citizen. He quailed before the faction of Clodius; was mean towards Cæsar; as a friend, could never be trusted. Cicero entertains no doubt that he would, if victorious, have renewed the proscriptions of Sylla."—*Niebuhr.*

Julius Cæsar was one of the greatest leaders of any age. In war he was always successful. As a statesman he gave evidence of foresight and wisdom. He was foully murdered in the senate house by the patrician party led by Brutus and Cassius, 44 B.C.

"Goethe says somewhere that the murder of Cæsar was the most senseless act that the Romans ever committed, and a truer word was never spoken."—*Niebuhr.*

Mark Antony, on the death of Cæsar, became leader of the friends of the murdered hero. He became a member of the second triumvirate, and was a brilliant general. His love of sensuous enjoyment was his weakness. He incurred the enmity of Octavianus Cæsar by neglecting his wife, Octavia, the sister of Octavianus, for Cleopatra. After the defeat at Actium, 31 B.C., Antony and Cleopatra both committed suicide.

"If we compare Antony with Octavian, we must say that Antony was open-hearted; whereas Octavian was made up of hypocrisy: his whole life was a farce. It is well-known that on his death-bed at Nola, he asked his friends whether he had not played the comedy of his life well? He was an actor throughout his life, and everything he did was a farce, well devised and skilfully executed. The most profound hypocrisy was his greatest talent. In the vicious and profligate life of Antony, on the other hand, there occur some actions which show good nature, generosity, and even greatness."—*Niebuhr.*

Octavianus Cæsar. (Augustus.) Adopted son of Julius Cæsar. Only eighteen years old when Cæsar was assassinated. Came at once to Rome to claim his inheritance. He won favor with the people, and soon became the rival of Antony. With Antony and Lepidus he formed the second triumvirate. After the death of Lepidus he shared the control of the empire with Antony till B.C. 31. He then became supreme ruler (Imperator). Under him Rome reached its greatest splendor. He was an excellent politician and a great commander. For forty-five years he was the mightiest Roman.

Virgil, the greatest epic poet of Rome, flourished during the period of Octavian. Born 70 B.C., died 19 B.C. His chief works were the Bucolics, Georgica and Æneid.

Horace, born 65 B.C., died 8 B.C. A great lyric poet. His chief works were his Odes and Epistles. He was a republican in sentiment, and fought with Brutus at Philippi.

Sallust, born 86 B.C., died 34 B.C. First great Roman historian, wrote the Catalina and the Jugurtha, and the Historiarum Libri Quinque. Fought under Cæsar in Africa. Made governor of Numidia.

Ovid, born 43 B.C., died 18 A.D. A poet who was also a magistrate. Wrote Metamorphosis, Fasti and Tristia.

Livy, born 59 B.C., died 17 A.D., was Rome's great historian. His chief work was The History of Rome, comprising 142 books.

2. The First Triumvirate.

Formed 60 B.C. Cæsar commanded in the west, Pompey remained at Rome, and Crassus went to Syria. Crassus died 53 B.C. Pompey and Cæsar became rivals. Pompey was jealous of Cæsar's great successes in Gaul and Britain. The senate, led by Cato, took the side of Pompey. Cæsar was ordered to give up his command in 49 B.C. He refused unless Pompey would resign too. The senate declined Cæsar's offer and he marched to Italy, crossed the Rubicon, and renewed his offer. The senate again rejected it. In sixty days Cæsar was master of Italy. Pompey left Italy. Battle of Pharsalia, 48 B.C. Defeat of Pompey, who fled to Egypt, and was there murdered. Cæsar dictator, 48 B.C. (he had been dictator for eleven days in 49 B.C.) till the end of 46 B.C. Subdued opposition in Asia and Africa. Was reappointed dictator third time and consul fourth time in 45 B.C. Dictator fourth time and consul fifth time, 44 B.C.

Was offered the crown, but rejected it. Murdered on Ide's of March, 44 B.C., by a conspiracy of sixty republicans led by Brutus and Cassius.

3. **Second Triumvirate.**

Antony drove the conspirators from Italy. Octavianus, Cæsar's adopted son, claimed to be Cæsar's heir, and was chosen by the senate to break the power of Antony. He suddenly changed his plan, and united with Antony and Lepidus to form the second triumvirate. The triumviri proscribed 2,000 equites and 300 senators. Each named his own personal enemies. Cicero was named by Antony, against whom he had uttered his Philippics. Brutus and Cassius defeated by Antony and Octavius at Philippi, 42 B.C. Antony went to Asia and Egypt. Cleopatra. Octavius strengthened himself at Rome. In 40 B.C. Antony and Octavius quarreled, but Antony married Octavia, sister of Octavius, and the breach was healed. In 37 B.C. the triumvirate was prolonged for five years. In 36 B.C. Lepidus attempted to resist Octavius, and was banished. In 32 Octavius declared war against Antony, who had divorced Octavia and neglected his duties under the influence of Cleopatra. Antony and Cleopatra defeated at Actium, 31 B.C. Death of Antony and Cleopatra. Octavius left in sole control, 31 B.C.

4. **Constitutional Development.**

The republic overthrown by military commanders. Republicans murdered Julius Cæsar to avoid a monarchy, which they believed he intended to establish. They were themselves driven from Rome, and afterwards defeated. Octavius finally secured supreme power, but used it in a constitutional way. He was able to give Rome the needed rest from turmoil and political revolution which had slowly and surely led to the decline of the republican spirit.

He restored order throughout the empire.

He organized a thorough system of provincial governments.

He gave new dignity to the Senate and the Equites.

5. **Wars from 60 B.C. to 14 A.D.**

   (a) **Cæsar's Campaigns in Gaul and Britain, 58 to 50 B C.**

   For eight years Cæsar remained in Gaul, subduing the tribes and establishing Roman authority. In the first year he drove the Helvetii and Suevi out of Gaul and subdued Southern Gaul. He conquered the north in 57 B C. and the west in 56 B.C. In 55 and 54 B.C. he invaded Germany and Britain. In the latter part of 54 and during the next two years he was occupied in subduing a general revolt of the Gauls. In 52 B.C. he was at first defeated by a great warrior, Vercingetorix, but after being in the greatest possible danger his military genius saved his army and conquered his greatest foe. In eight campaigns, according to Plutarch, Cæsar took more than 800 cities, defeated 300 nations, and fought against 3,000,000 of men, of whom he slew 1,000,000 and took another million prisoners.

   (b) **Parthian Wars.**

   The Parthians were the greatest rivals of Rome for the supremacy of Western Asia. Crassus was defeated and his army destroyed at Carrhæ, 53 B.C.

   (c) **Civil war between Cæsar and Pompey.**

   Pompey favorite of the Senate. Cæsar ordered to resign his command. refused to do so. Marched to Rome. Flight of Pompey. Cæsar victorious at Pharsalia, 48 B.C. Pompey murdered as he was landing in Egypt.

   (d) **Cæsar's conquests in Asia, Africa and Spain.**

   During the years 47, 46 and 45 B.C. Cæsar was fully occupied in quelling revolts and organizing the empire in Egypt, Asia, Northern Africa and Spain.

   (e) **Civil war between the Second Triumvirate and the Republicans.**

   The republicans, led by Brutus and Cassius, were defeated by Antony and Octavius at Philippi, 42 B.C.

(f) War between the East and West.

Antony in the East and Octavius in the West declared war against each other, 32 B.C. Defeat of Antony and Cleopatra at Actium, 31 B.C.

(g) Northern Wars.

Pannonia had been conquered by Octavius, 30 B.C., but it revolted in 12 B.C. The country now called Germany attracted the attention of Octavius about the same time. Two armies were sent out, one against Germany under Drusus, and the other against Pannonia, under Tiberius. Drusus and Tiberius were sons of Livia, the wife of Octavius, by a former husband. During his fourth campaign Drusus died, but Tiberius took his place and conducted the war against Germany for two years more.

In 1 A.D. the German war began again, and lasted till 6 A.D., when Tiberius concluded a treaty with the Germans in order to quell a revolt of the Pannonians. In 9 A.D. the Pannonian war ended in favor of Rome. In the same year the Germans in the northwest, near Gaul, rebelled and destroyed the Roman army under Varus. Tiberius again invaded Germany, by way of Gaul, and in 11 A.D. he crossed Germany unopposed.

7. General Progress.

During the reign of Augustus (Octavius) the organization of twenty-eight new provinces, and the taxes and trade with the various parts of the empire, which practically embraced the whole of the known world, brought great wealth to Rome. Augustus ornamented the city, and became the patron of literature and art. The internal peace which he was able to maintain gave the people time to devote to general culture and social development.

The first public library was opened in Rome B.C. 37. The Augustan half century was Rome's brightest era.

KEY TO MAP OF BATTLEFIELDS

AND HISTORICAL PLACES IN ENGLAND

BATTLEFIELDS.

(1) Bannockburn.
(2) Barnet.
(3) Bosworth Field.
(4) Bothwell Bridge.
(5) Dunkirk.
(6) Edgehill.
(7) Evesham.
(8) Falkirk.
(9) Flodden.
(10) Halidon Hill.
(11) Hastings (Senlac).
(12) Lewes.
(13) Marston Moor.
(14) Mortimer's Cross.
(15) Naseby.
(16) Neville's Cross.
(17) Otterburn.
(18) Preston Pans.
(19) Sedgmoor.
(20) St. Albans.
(21) Tewkesbury.
(22) Towton.
(23) Wakefield.
(24) Worcester.

HISTORICAL PLACES.

(25) Cambridge.
(26) Dover.
(27) Oxford.
(28) Runnymede.
(29) Plymouth.
(30) Portsmouth.
(31) Torbay.
(32) York.

English and Canadian History Note Book.

GAGE'S
New Topical English and Canadian History Note Book.

This little Primer is prepared to cover the Public School History Course in English and Canadian History, and is printed so as to furnish a number of blank leaves to allow students to make additional notes. PRICE 25 CENTS.

LEADING FEATURES.

The Notes.
The Notes are arranged Topically under such headings as best indicate the True Growth of the nation.

Progress of the People.
The Progress of the People, the Struggle for Freedom the Establishment of Representative Government, and the Development of Education, Literature, and Religion, are given more prominence than wars.

Colonial Extension.
The Colonial Extension of the British Empire is briefly outlined.

The History is Classified.
The whole History is Classified, so that the Relationships of the Great Upward Movement can be understood.

English and Canadian History Note Book.

Arrangement of the Notes.

The Arrangement of the Notes makes it Easy, Definite, and thorough reviewing, perfectly simple without a teacher.

Admirable Preparation.

The Notes supply an admirable preparation for the study of larger histories, and the best means for clearly remembering what has been learned from them.

Additional Notes.

Ample space has been left for additional notes to be written by the student.

Used in Connection with any History.

The Notes can be used in connection with any History and are intended to stimulate the further study of the important subject with which they treat.

By the Use of this Note Book :

1. *Time is saved to Teachers and Pupils.*

2. *Success at Examinations made more certain.*

3. *Interest is awakened in the Study of History.*

4. *A simple, definity Method of studying History is revealed.*

W. J. GAGE & CO.'S PUBLICATIONS

GAGE'S
English & Canadian History Note Book.

From PROF. WILLIAM CLARK, M.A., LL.D.,
Trinity College, Toronto.

"It is an admirable compilation, equally useful to lecturer and student, and I am very glad to peruse it. I shall often refer to it."

A long-felt want.

Your English and Canadian History Notes fill a long felt want. There seems to be no text book at present suitable for junior pupils and the notes will save the teacher much time in arranging class work. They are just the thing for oral teaching and review, and may be used with any English or Canadian History.—W. A. GRAHAM, *Prin. Oil Springs P.S.*

A very great aid.

Your Notes on English and Canadian History will meet the needs of many teachers who are pressed for time. Entrance pupils will find it a very great aid.—L. F. HANKOP, *Prin. Niagara Falls P.S.*

Admirably adapted.

It is admirably adapted for Entrance classes, and will make the work definite and thorough.—S. Y. TAYLOR, *Prin. Public School, Paris.*

Just the thing.

I am pleased when I see your "English and Canadian History Note book" in the hands of my pupils. Some of them are using them with their regular text-books and find them just the thing.—G. E. HENDERSON, *Principal Public School, Kingsville.*

Great help to students of history.

I have examined your Canadian and English History Note Book, and, although I am somewhat prejudiced against Notes Books of any kind I must say that yours is the best and most carefully arranged Notes that I have seen coming from the press, and unless the use of a judicious teacher they must be a great help to students of history.—THOS. HAMMOND, *H.M. teacher P.S.*

Grasping points supplied.

The History Note I am sure cannot fail to meet the approval of teachers, especially in the public school, where the leading facts of Canadian and English History are required. This little book is admirably adapted to the needs of the teacher, since History can be learned by young pupils only by providing them with grasping points clustered, they may retain the hold they got during a lesson, and your book supplied these points.—J. H. KILMAN, *Edgemere P.S.*

Fill an important niche in review.

I expect to find the Note on History fill an important niche in the review lessons on English History.—M. WATSON, *M.A., Head Master, Prescott.*

W. J. Gage & Co.'s Publications.

PROBLEMS IN ARITHMETIC
FOR PUBLIC SCHOOLS.
By CHAS. CLARKSON, B.A., Principal Seaforth Collegiate Inst.

- - PREPARED FOR - -

SENIOR CLASSES,
 ENTRANCE EXAMINATION,
  PUBLIC SCHOOL LEAVING,
   PRIMARY EXAMINATION.

The Laboratory Plan Applied to Arithmetic.

Practical Help for Busy Teachers.

SCHOLARS' EDITION CONTAINS

INTRODUCTION and REVIEW QUESTIONS — 16 pages practical suggestions and selected review questions.
ENTRANCE EXAMINATION PAPERS—Complete, 1873 to 1892.
PUBLIC SCHOOL LEAVING PAPERS—Set of 14 papers.
TYPE SOLUTIONS—20 pages of great variety.
PRIMARY EXAMINATION PAPERS—1873 to 1892.

PRICE, - 30 CENTS.

TEACHERS' EDITION CONTAINS

ANSWERS TO ALL THE PROBLEMS, and
SKELETON SOLUTIONS to several hundreds of the problems; short, clear, useful in the class-room.

PRICE, - 60 CENTS.

A PRACTICAL BOOK THAT WILL HELP YOU.

The W. J. Gage Co.'s Publications

THE PUBLIC SCHOOL ALGEBRA
ON THE
INDUCTIVE METHOD

BY

C. CLARKSON, B.A., Prin. Coll. Institute, Stratford, Ont.

In considering an introductory series of developmental lessons to form a guide to good teaching and a thorough introduction to larger work, all doubts are, all explanations of merely mechanical matters, and all simple examples worked up to trouble are omitted. These sections leading to the ideas are puzzling and to a first book of algebra it is more particularly unknown to print long explanations, for they are never read by junior pupils. The answers are the only parts of much consequence to the learner, and accordingly this book contains almost wholly of exercises. The pupils' previous knowledge of arithmetic is a sufficient basis and a long list of abstract definitions is entirely unnecessary. In a properly graded set of questions the pupil is led to discover for himself and make his own generalizations. He is led to evolve algebra out of arithmetic by carefully constructed and finely graded exercises, inductive questions, comparisons, etc.

The guiding principles of the book are these:
1. Follow the line of least resistance.
2. Seek practical applications from the beginning.
3. Connect arithmetic and algebra as closely as possible.
4. Introduce simple tests of accuracy wherever possible.
5. Avoid all difficult examples.
6. Grade the steps very carefully.
7. Supply abundance of review work and repeat the same idea under various forms.
8. Pay no attention to the traditional order of introducing the topics. Select the easier first. Postpone all difficulties to a later stage.
9. Supply a treasury of practical examples containing a rich variety of questions.

The plan of the book is entirely original. The development of the subject is the simplest yet discovered and the progress of the pupil is proportionally rapid. The first fifty pages contain as much as is usually given in 150 of the common text-books. This book is solid matter. No space lost on definitions and superfluous explanations.

SHORT CLEAR HINTS AND SUGGESTIONS

to all the harder examples show the pupil how to begin and what to aim at. The examples are so arranged that the pupil has to work out his own education, but he is not left without sufficient help to prevent him from making unnecessary errors of the ever hard to solve.

There is no other text book that can rival the Public School Algebra as an introductory text book. It has been prepared with a view to meet precisely the pedagogical standard for FORWARD EXAMINATIONS of PUBLIC SCHOOLS. It will be found right up to the requirements of the new Courses.

It is Condensed, Original, Helpful, and will win its way wherever it is tried.

W. J. GAGE & CO.'S PUBLICATIONS.

Virgil Ænid. Book I.

With Notes and Vocabulary by J. E. WETHERELL, B.A. Contains Introduction, Notes, Synopsis, Examination Questions, Vocabulary, Miscellaneous Index of proper names. Price 30 cents.

This is the cheapest volume published of Virgil Book I. with Vocabulary.

Best school edition.
It is the best school edition of Virgil I have seen.— A. W. BANNISER, B.A., *High Classical School Master, Farmersville.*

A model text-book.
It is quite a model text-book.—S. F. MCGILLIVRAY, B.A., *H.M. H.S., Fergus, Ont.*

A most valuable book.
I consider the book a most valuable one for young students.—WM. TASSIE, M.A., LL.D., *H.M. Coll. Inst., Peterboro.*

Shall recommend it.
I consider it the most complete edition I have seen. I shall recommend it to my pupils. — A. G. KNIGHT, M.A., *H.S., Deseronto.*

Virgil Ænid. Book II.

Edited by J. C. ROBERTSON, B.A., Classical Master, Owen Sound Collegiate Institute, Editor of Cæsar III. and IV., and one of the editors of Robertson and Carruther's New Authorized Latin Book.

Leading Features.—1. *Introduction:* Clear and readable, and written for the capacity of those who will use the book. The section on the metre made particularly clear.

2. *Notes.*—Entirely devoted to (a) clearing away the difficulties the average young student would find; (b) leading the student to look upon the poem as a piece of literature, to be understood and appreciated. All notes that would be above the pupils' heads are avoided.

3. *References* on difficult points are given to the standard and authorized Grammars, but these are purely supplementary, the notes being as a rule complete in themselves.

4. *Vocabulary.*—Specially prepared for this edition.

5. *Illustrations.* Intended to make the pupils' conception of the story more vivid, and increase his interest in it.

6. *Accuracy* in typography, annotations and vocabulary.

www.ingramcontent.com/pod-product-compliance
Lightning Source LLC
Chambersburg PA
CBHW022142160426
43197CB00009B/1397